Rick Steves'

POCKET

ATHENS

Rick Steves with Gene Openshaw
and Cameron Hewitt

Contents

Introduction

Traveling to Athens is like making a pilgrimage to the cradle of our civilization. Romantics can't help but get goose bumps as they kick around the same pebbles that once stuck in Socrates' sandals, with the floodlit Parthenon forever floating ethereally overhead. You'll walk in the footsteps of the great minds that created democracy, philosophy, theater, and more... even when you're dodging motorcycles on "pedestrianized" streets.

While sprawling and congested, the city has a compact, user-friendly tourist zone, with sights such as the Acropolis Museum and the Ancient Agora an easy walk apart. Many locals speak English, major landmarks are well-signed, and most street signs are in both Greek and English.

Introduction

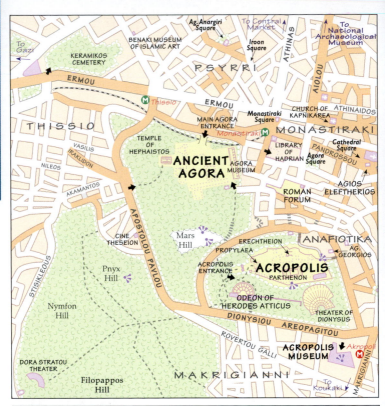

To Gazi

KERAMIKOS CEMETERY

BENAKI MUSEUM OF ISLAMIC ART

Ag. Anargiri Square

To Central Market

Iroon Square

To National Archaeological Museum

PSYRRI

ERMOU

ATHINAS

AIOLOU

Thissio

ERMOU

ATHINAIDOS

THISSIO

VASILIS

IRAKLIDON

NILEOS

AKAMANTOS

TEMPLE OF HEPHAISTOS

MAIN AGORA ENTRANCE

Monastiraki Square

Monastiraki

CHURCH OF KAPNIKAREA

MONASTIRAKI

ANCIENT AGORA

AGORA MUSEUM

LIBRARY OF HADRIAN

Agora Square

PANDROSSOU

Cathedral Square

ROMAN FORUM

AGIOS ELEFTHERIOS

APOSTOLOU PAVLOU

CINE THESEION

Mars Hill

ERECHTHEION

PROPYLAEA

ANAFIOTIKA

AG. GEORGIOS

Pnyx Hill

ACROPOLIS ENTRANCE

ACROPOLIS

PARTHENON

STISIKLEOUS

Nymfon Hill

ODEON OF HERODES ATTICUS

THEATER OF DIONYSUS

DIONYSIOU AREOPAGITOU

ROVERTOU GALLI

ACROPOLIS MUSEUM

Akropoli

DORA STRATOU THEATER

Filopappos Hill

MAKRIGIANNI

MAKRIGIANNI

To Koukaki

Map Legend

⚲	Viewpoint		Area of Ancient Ruins		Park
↑	Entrance	Ⓣ	Taxi Stand	Ⓟ	Parking
WC	Restroom	ⓂⓂⓂ	Metro Stop		Tourist Info
⌂	Church	Ⓑ	Bus Stop	▪	Statue/Point of Interest

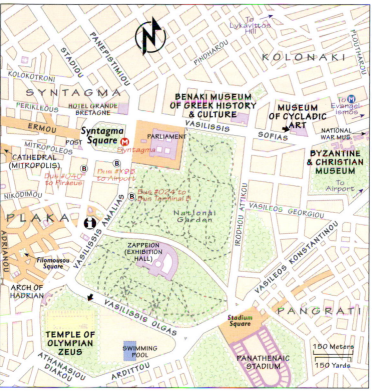

KOLONAKI

To Lykavittós Hill

PINDHAROU

PANEPISTIMIOU

STADIOU

KOLOKOTRONI

SYNTAGMA

PERIKLEOUS

HOTEL GRANDE BRETAGNE

BENAKI MUSEUM OF GREEK HISTORY & CULTURE

MUSEUM OF CYCLADIC ART

To Evangel-ismos

ERMOU

Syntagma Square

PARLIAMENT

VASILISSIS

SOFIAS

MITROPOLEOS

POST

Syntagma

BYZANTINE & CHRISTIAN MUSEUM

NATIONAL WAR MUS.

CATHEDRAL (MITROPOLIS)

Bus #040 to Piraeus

Bus #X95 to Airport

To Airport

NIKODIMOU

Bus #024 to Bus Terminal B

IRODHOU ATTIKOU

VASILEOS GEORGIOU

PLAKA

VASILISSIS AMALIAS

National Garden

VASILEOS KONSTANTINOU

ADRIANOU

Filomousou Square

ZAPPEION (EXHIBITION HALL)

PANGRATI

ARCH OF HADRIAN

VASILISSIS OLGAS

Stadium Square

TEMPLE OF OLYMPIAN ZEUS

SWIMMING POOL

PANATHENAIC STADIUM

150 Meters

150 Yards

ATHANASIOU DIAKOU

ARDITTOU

Tunnel	**Metro Line**
Pedestrian Zone	**Stairs**
Railway	**Walk/Tour Route**
Ferry/Boat Route	**Trail**

Use this legend to help you navigate the maps in this book.

About This Book

The core of the book is five self-guided tours that zero in on Athens' greatest sights. My Athens City Walk leads you on a three-part stroll through the engaging and refreshingly small city center. My Acropolis and Ancient Agora tours take you back in time to the bustling religious and commercial centers of ancient Greece. And the Acropolis Museum and National Archaeological Museum provide up-close views of artifacts and treasures unearthed from Greece's great ancient sites.

The rest of the book is a traveler's tool kit. You'll find plenty more about Athens' attractions, from shopping to nightlife to less touristy sights. And there are helpful hints on saving money, avoiding crowds, getting around on public transportation, enjoying a great meal, and more.

Athens by Neighborhood

Ninety-five percent of Athens is noisy, polluted modern sprawl, jammed with characterless concrete suburbs—poorly planned and hastily erected

Key to This Book

Sights are rated:

▲▲▲	Don't miss
▲▲	Try hard to see
▲	Worthwhile if you can make it
No rating	Worth knowing about

Tourist information offices are abbreviated as **TI,** and bathrooms are **WCs.**

Like Europe, this book uses the **24-hour clock.** It's the same through 12:00 noon, then keep going: 13:00 (1:00 p.m.), 14:00 (2:00 p.m.), and so on.

For **opening times,** if a sight is listed as "May-Oct daily 9:00-16:00," it should be open from 9 a.m. until 4 p.m. from the first day of May until the last day of October (but expect exceptions).

For **updates** to this book, visit www.ricksteves.com/update. For a valuable list of reports and experiences—good and bad—from fellow travelers, check www.ricksteves.com/feedback.

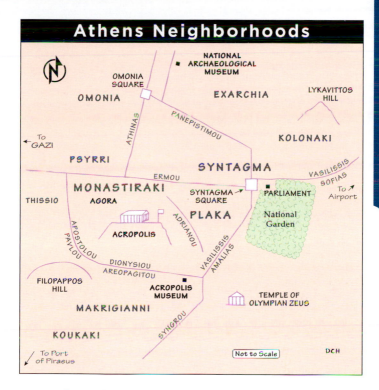

Athens Neighborhoods

to house the area's rapidly expanding population. But most visitors never see that part of Athens. Almost everything of importance to tourists is within a few blocks of the Acropolis.

A good map is a necessity for enjoying Athens on foot. The fine map the tourist info office (TI) gives out works great. You'll concentrate on the following districts:

The Plaka (PLAH-kah, Πλάκα in Greek): This neighborhood at the foot of the Acropolis is the core of the tourist's Athens. One of the only parts of town that's atmospheric and Old World-feeling, it's also the most crassly touristic (souvenir shops and tacky tavernas).

Athens at a Glance

Confirm hours locally.

▲▲▲**Acropolis** The most important ancient sights in the Western world, where Athenians built their architectural masterpiece—the Parthenon. **Hours:** Daily May-mid-Sept 8:00-20:00, mid-Sept-Oct until 18:00, Nov-April until 17:00. See page 41.

▲▲▲**Acropolis Museum** Glassy modern temple for ancient art. **Hours:** Tue-Sun 8:00-20:00, Fri until 22:00, closed Mon. See page 87.

▲▲▲**Ancient Agora** Social and commercial center of ancient Athens, with a well-preserved temple and intimate museum. **Hours:** Daily May-Aug 8:00-20:00, Sept until 18:45, Oct until 18:00, Nov-April until 15:00, museum opens Mon at 11:00. See page 69.

▲▲▲**National Archaeological Museum** World's best collection of ancient Greek art. **Hours:** May-mid-Sept Tue-Sun 8:00-20:00, Mon 13:30-20:00; mid-Sept-Oct Tue-Sun 8:00-19:00, Mon 13:30-20:00; Nov-April Tue-Sun 8:00-15:00, Mon 13:30-20:00. See page 99.

▲▲**"Acropolis Loop"** Traffic-free pedestrian walkways ringing the Acropolis with vendors, cafés, and special events. **Hours:** Always open. See page 122.

▲▲**Temple of Olympian Zeus** Remains of the largest temple in ancient Greece. **Hours:** Daily 8:00-20:00, Sept until 19:00, off-season until 17:00. See page 127.

Monastiraki (mah-nah-stee-RAH-kee, Μοναστηρακι): This area ("Little Monastery") borders the Plaka to the northwest, surrounding the square of the same name. It has a handy Metro stop (where line 1/green meets line 3/blue), seedy flea market, and souvlaki stands.

Psyrri (psee-REE, Ψυρή): Formerly a dumpy ghetto just north of Monastiraki, Psyrri is now a cutting-edge nightlife and dining district—and one of central Athens' most appealing areas to explore after dark.

Syntagma (seen-DOG-mah, Συνταγμα): Centered on Athens' main square, Syntagma ("Constitution") Square, this urban-feeling zone melts into the Plaka to the south and is bounded to the east by the Parliament building and the National Garden. While the Plaka is dominated by tourist shops, Syntagma is where local urbanites do their shopping.

▲▲**Benaki Museum of Greek History and Culture** Exquisite collection of artifacts from the ancient, Byzantine, Ottoman, and modern eras. **Hours:** Wed-Sat 9:00-17:00, Thu until 24:00, Sun 9:00-15:00, closed Mon-Tue. See page 130.

▲▲**Museum of Cycladic Art** World's largest compilation of Cycladic art, from 4,000 years ago. **Hours:** Mon and Wed-Sat 10:00-17:00, Thu until 20:00, Sun 11:00-17:00, closed Tue. See page 131.

▲▲**Byzantine and Christian Museum** Fascinating look at the Byzantines, who put their own stamp on a flourishing culture. **Hours:** Tue-Sun 9:00-16:00, closed Mon. See page 132.

▲**Mars Hill** Historic spot—with a classic view of the Acropolis—where the Apostle Paul preached to the Athenians. **Hours:** Always open. See page 122.

▲**Syntagma Square** Athens' most famous public space, with a popular changing-of-the-guard ceremony. **Hours:** Always open, guards change five minutes before the top of each hour, full ceremony with marching band most Sun at 11:00. See page 125.

▲**Panathenaic (a.k.a. "Olympic") Stadium** Gleaming marble stadium restored to its second-century A.D. condition. **Hours:** Daily March-Oct 8:00-19:00, Nov-Feb 8:00-17:00. See page 128.

Thissio (thee-SEE-oh, Θησείο): West of the Ancient Agora, Thissio is an upscale, local-feeling residential neighborhood with piles of outdoor cafés and restaurants. It's easily accessible thanks to the handy pedestrian walkway around the Acropolis.

Makrigianni (mah-kree-YAH-nee, Μακρυγιάννη) and **Koukaki** (koo-KAH-kee, Κουκάκι): Tucked just behind (south of) the Acropolis, these overlapping urban neighborhoods have a lived-in charm and make a good home base.

Kolonaki (koh-loh-NAH-kee, Κολωνάκι): Just north and east of the Parliament/Syntagma Square area, this upscale diplomatic quarter, with several good museums and a yuppie dining zone, huddles under the tall, pointy Lykavittos Hill.

Daily Reminder

Sunday: Most sights are open, but the Art Tower and Central Market are closed. The Monastiraki flea market is best to visit today. An elaborate changing of the guard—including a marching band—sometimes takes place at 11:00 in front of the Parliament building. Off-season (Nov-March), the Acropolis is free on first Sunday.

Monday: Many museums and galleries are closed, including the Acropolis Museum, Benaki Museum of Greek History and Culture, Benaki Museum of Islamic Art, Byzantine and Christian Museum, Art Tower, and National War Museum. The National Archaeological Museum opens at 13:30, and the Agora Museum opens at 11:00.

Tuesday: These sights are closed today: the Museum of Cycladic Art, Art Tower, and Benaki Museum of Greek History and Culture.

Wednesday-Saturday: All major sights are open.

Evening Sightseeing: In summer, these places stay open daily until 20:00: the Acropolis, Ancient Agora, National Archaeological Museum, Temple of Olympian Zeus, and the Byzantine and Christian Museum. Some sights are open until 20:00 year-round, including the cathedral (daily), Acropolis Museum (Tue-Sun; Fri until 22:00), Art Tower (Wed-Fri), and Museum of Cycladic Art (Thu only). The Benaki Museum of Islamic Art is open Wednesday until 21:00, and the Benaki Museum of Greek History and Culture is open Thursday until 24:00.

Major Streets: The Acropolis is ringed by a broad traffic-free walkway, named **Dionysiou Areopagitou** (Διονυσιου Αρεοπαγιτου) to the south and **Apostolou Pavlou** (Αποστολου Παυλου) to the west; for simplicity, I call these the **"Acropolis Loop."** Touristy **Adrianou** street (Αδριανου) curves through the Plaka a few blocks away from the Acropolis' base. Partly pedestrianized **Ermou** street (Ερμου) runs west from Syntagma Square, defining the Plaka, Monastiraki, and Thissio to the south, and Psyrri to the north. Where Ermou meets Monastiraki, **Athinas** street (Αθηνας) heads north to Omonia Square.

Planning Your Time

The Acropolis/Ancient Agora, the Acropolis Museum, and the National Archaeological Museum deserve a half-day each. Two days' total is plenty of time for the casual tourist to see the city's main attractions.

Day 1: In the morning, follow my Athens City Walk. Grab a souvlaki lunch near Monastiraki, and spend midday in the markets (shopping in the Plaka, browsing in the Central Market, and wandering through the flea market—best on Sun). After lunch, as the crowds (and heat) subside, visit the ancient biggies: First tour the Ancient Agora, then hike up to the Acropolis (carefully confirming how late the Acropolis is open). Be the last person off the Acropolis. Stroll down the Dionysiou Areopagitou pedestrian boulevard, then promenade to dinner—in Thissio, Monastiraki, Psyrri, or the Plaka.

Day 2: Spend the morning visiting the Acropolis Museum and exploring the Plaka. After lunch, head to the National Archaeological Museum (note that on Mondays, the Acropolis Museum is closed and the National Archaeological Museum opens at 13:30).

Day 3 and Beyond: Head out to Kolonaki to take in some of Athens' lesser sights—the Benaki Museum of Greek History and Culture, Museum of Cycladic Art, and Byzantine and Christian Museum. Or consider ditching Athens for a long but satisfying side-trip to Delphi, a sweet getaway to the isle of Hydra, or a quick dip into the Peloponnese peninsula, with the charming port town of Nafplio and the famous ancient sights of Epidavros and Mycenae. Even better, spend the night.

These are busy day-plans, so be sure to schedule in slack time for picnics, laundry, people-watching, leisurely dinners, shopping, and recharging your touristic batteries. Slow down and be open to unexpected

experiences and the hospitality of the Greek people.

Trip Tips: The Acropolis ticket gives you entry to Athens' major ancient sites, including the Acropolis and Ancient Agora (see page 123 for more info).

Don't put off visiting a must-see sight—in Greece, you never know when a place will change its hours or close because of a strike, budget cut, restoration project, or unforeseen circumstance (such as rockslides at Delphi). Confirm hours carefully. Many museums have shorter hours around the Easter holiday.

Download my free Athens audio tours—covering the Acropolis, Ancient Agora, National Archaeological Museum, and Athens City Walk—onto your mobile device and bring them along (see page 168). For more sightseeing tips, see page 167.

A word about travel safety: Because of Greece's "economic meltdown," there have been many demonstrations and occasional riots—which have sometimes turned violent. These tend to be isolated and are unlikely to affect travelers or the main tourist attractions.

I hope you have a great trip! Traveling like a temporary local and taking advantage of the information here, you'll enjoy the absolute most out of every mile, minute, and euro. I'm happy that you'll be visiting places I know and love, and meeting some of my favorite Greek people.

Happy travels! *Kalo taxidi!*

Athens City Walk

From Syntagma Square to Monastiraki Square

This walk takes you through the striking contrasts of the city center—from chaotic, traffic-clogged urban zones, to sleepy streets packed with bearded priests shopping for a new robe or chalice, to peaceful back lanes barely wide enough for a donkey that twist their way up toward the Acropolis. The walk begins at Syntagma Square, meanders through the fascinating old Plaka district, and finishes at lively Monastiraki Square (near the Ancient Agora, markets, good restaurants, and a handy Metro stop). This sightseeing spine will help you get a once-over-lightly look at Athens, which you can use as a springboard for diving into the city's various colorful sights and neighborhoods.

ORIENTATION

Churches: Athens' churches keep irregular hours, but they're generally open daily 8:30-13:30 & 17:00-19:30. If you want to buy candles at churches (as the locals do), be sure to have a few small coins.

Cathedral: Generally open daily 8:00-13:00 & 16:30-20:00, no afternoon closure in summer.

Temple of Olympian Zeus: €2, covered by Acropolis ticket, daily 8:00-20:00, Sept until 19:00, off-season until 17:00, Vasilissis Olgas 1, Metro line 2/red: Akropoli, tel. 210-922-6330, www.culture.gr.

Roman Forum: €2, covered by Acropolis ticket, daily 8:00-19:00, Sept until 18:30, off-season until 15:00, corner of Pelopida and Aiolou streets, Metro line 1/green or 3/blue: Monastiraki, tel. 210-324-5220, www.culture.gr.

When to Go: Do this walk early in your visit, as it can help you get your bearings in this potentially confusing city. Mornings are best, since many churches close for an afternoon break and other sights—such as the Acropolis—are too crowded to enjoy.

Dress Code: Wearing shorts inside churches (especially the cathedral) is frowned upon, though usually tolerated.

Getting There: The walk begins at Syntagma Square, just northeast of the Plaka tourist zone. It's a short walk from my recommended Plaka hotels; if you're staying away from the city center, get here by Metro (line 2/red or line 3/blue to Syntagma stop).

Audio Tour: You can download a free audio version of this tour for your mobile device via www.ricksteves.com/audioeurope, iTunes, or the Rick Steves Audio Europe smartphone app.

Length of This Walk: Allow plenty of time. This three-part walk takes two hours without stops or detours. But if you explore and dip into sights here and there—pausing to ponder a dimly lit Orthodox church, or doing some window (or actual) shopping—it can enjoyably eat up a half-day or more. If you find this walk too long, it's easy to break up—stop after Part 2 and return for Part 3 at a different time or on another day.

Starring: Athens' top squares, churches, and Roman ruins, connected by bustling urban streets that are alternately choked with cars and mopeds, or thronged by pedestrians, vendors...and fellow tourists.

THE WALK BEGINS

This lengthy walk is thematically divided into three parts: The first part focuses on modern Athens, centered on Syntagma Square and the Ermou shopping street. The second part focuses on Athens' Greek Orthodox faith, with visits to three different but equally interesting churches. And the third part is a wander through the charming old core of Athens, including the touristy Plaka and the mellow Greek-village-on-a-hillside of Anafiotika.

PART 1: MODERN ATHENS

This part of our walk lets you feel the pulse of a European capital.

▶ *Start at Syntagma Square. From the leafy park at the center of the square, climb to the top of the stairs (in the middle of the square) and stand across the street from the big, Neoclassical Greek Parliament building.*

❶ Syntagma Square (Plateia Syntagmatos)

As you look at posh hotels and major banks, you are standing atop the city's central Metro stop, surrounded by buses, cars, and taxis. Facing the Parliament building (east), get oriented to the square named for Greece's constitution (*syntagma;* seen-DOG-mah). From this point, sightseeing options spin off through the city like spokes on a wheel.

Fronting the square on the left (north) side are high-end hotels, including the opulent Hotel Grande Bretagne (with its swanky rooftop garden restaurant).

Directly to the left of the Parliament building is the head of Vasilissis Sofias avenue, lined with embassies and museums, including the Benaki Museum of Greek History and Culture, Museum of Cycladic Art, Byzantine and Christian Museum, and National War Museum. This boulevard leads to the ritzy Kolonaki quarter, with its funicular up to the top of Lykavittos Hill. Extending to the right of the Parliament building is the National Garden, Athens' "Central Park." Here you'll find the Zappeion mansion-turned-conference-hall (with a fine summer outdoor cinema nearby) and, beyond the greenery, the evocative, ancient Panathenaic Stadium.

On your right (south) is one of Athens' prime transit hubs, with stops for bus #X95 to the airport, bus #024 to Bus Terminal B/Liossion, and the

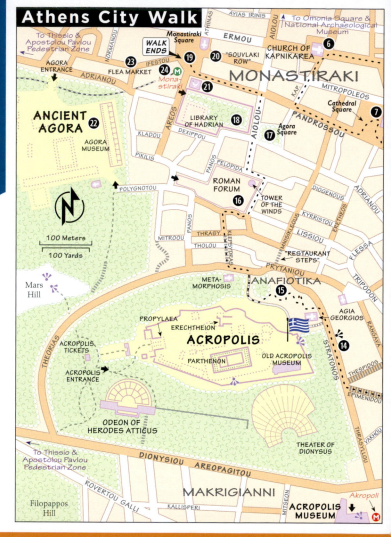

Athens City Walk

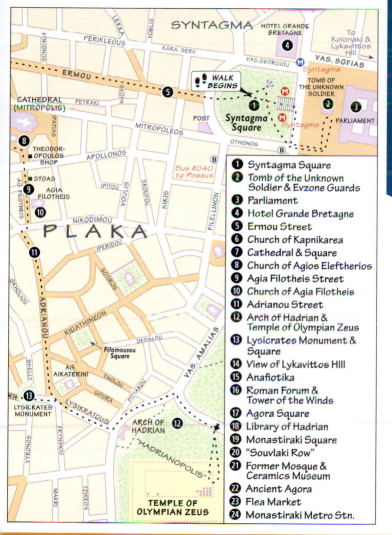

1 Syntagma Square
2 Tomb of the Unknown Soldier & Evzone Guards
3 Parliament
4 Hotel Grande Bretagne
5 Ermou Street
6 Church of Kapnikarea
7 Cathedral & Square
8 Church of Agios Eleftherios
9 Agia Filotheis Street
10 Church of Agia Filothei
11 Adrianou Street
12 Arch of Hadrian & Temple of Olympian Zeus
13 Lysicrates Monument & Square
14 View of Lykavittos Hill
15 Anafiotika
16 Roman Forum & Tower of the Winds
17 Agora Square
18 Library of Hadrian
19 Monastiraki Square
20 "Souvlaki Row"
21 Former Mosque & Ceramics Museum
22 Ancient Agora
23 Flea Market
24 Monastiraki Metro Stn.

Syntagma Square—center of modern Athens.

National Garden—Athens' Central Park.

Athens Coastal Tram. Beneath your feet is the Syntagma Metro station, the city's busiest. The TI is a few blocks away down busy Vasilissis Amalias street (beyond the tram terminus, not visible from here).

Behind you, at the west end of the square, stretches the traffic-free shopping street called Ermou, which heads to the Plaka neighborhood and Monastiraki Square. (We'll be heading that way soon.) Nearby is the terminus for one of Athens' two tourist trains (see page 171).

Plane trees (chosen for their resilience against pollution and the generous shade they provide) make Syntagma a breezy and restful spot. Breathe deep and ponder the fact that until 1990, Athens was the most polluted city in Europe. People advertising facial creams would put a mannequin outside on the street for three hours and film it turning black. The moral: You need our cream.

But over the last two decades, "green" policies have systematically cleaned up the air. Traffic, while still pretty extreme, is limited: Even- and odd-numbered license plates are prohibited in the center on alternate days. Check the license plates of passing cars (not taxis or motorcycles): The majority end with either an even or odd number, depending on the day of the week. Wealthy locals get around this restriction by owning two cars—one with even plates, the other with odd. While car traffic is down, motorcycle usage is up (since bikes are exempt). Central-heating fuel is more expensive and much cleaner these days (as required by European Union regulations), more of the city center is pedestrianized, and the city's public transport is top-notch.

▶ *Using the crosswalk (one on either side of Syntagma Square), cross the busy street. Directly in front of the Parliament you'll see the...*

❷ Tomb of the Unknown Soldier and the Evzone Guards

Standing amid pigeons and tourists in front of the imposing Parliament building, overlooking Syntagma Square, you're at the center of Athens' modern history. Above the simple marble-slab tomb—marked only with a cross—is a carved image of the Unknown Soldier, inspired by statues of ancient Greek warriors. Etched into the stone on each side of the tomb are the names of great battles in Greek military history from 1821 forward (practice your Greek alphabet by trying to read them: Cyprus, Korea, Rimini, Crete, and so on).

The tomb is guarded by the much-photographed evzone, an elite infantry unit of the Greek army. The guard changes five minutes before the top of each hour, with a less elaborate crossing of the guard on the half-hour. They march with a slow-motion, high-stepping march to their new positions, then stand ramrod straight, where you can pose alongside them. A full changing-of-the-guard ceremony, complete with marching band, takes place most Sundays at 11:00.

These colorful characters are clad in traditional pleated kilts *(fusta-nella)*, white britches, and pom-pom shoes. (The outfits may look a little goofy to a non-Greek, but their mothers and girlfriends are very proud.) The uniforms were made famous by the Klephts, ragtag bands of mountain guerrilla fighters. After nearly four centuries under the thumb of the Ottoman Empire (from today's Turkey, starting in 1453), the Greeks rose up. The Greek War of Independence (1821-1829) pitted the powerful Ottoman army against the lowly but wily Klephts. The Klephts reached back to their illustrious history, modeling their uniforms after those worn by soldiers from ancient Athens (the pom-poms date all the way back to the

Evzone guards at the tomb.

Their colorful outfits draw a crowd.

ancient Mycenaeans). The soldiers' winter skirts have 400 pleats...one for each year of Ottoman occupation (and don't you forget it). While considered heroes today for their courage and outrageous guerrilla tactics, the Klephts were once regarded as warlike bandits (their name shares a root with the English word "kleptomania").

As the Klephts and other Greeks fought for their independence, a number of farsighted Europeans (including the English poet Lord Byron)—inspired by the French Revolution and their own love of ancient Greek culture—came to their aid. In 1829, the rebels finally succeeded in driving their Ottoman rulers out of central Greece, and there was a movement to establish a modern democracy. However, the Greeks were unprepared to rule themselves, and so, after the Ottomans came...Otto.

▶ *For the rest of the story, take a step back for a view of the...*

❸ Parliament

The origins of this "palace of democracy" couldn't have been less democratic. The first independent Greek government, which had its capital in Nafplio, was too weak to be viable. As was standard operating procedure at that time, the great European powers forced Greece to accept a king from established European royalty.

In 1832, Prince Otto of Bavaria became King Otto of Greece. A decade later, after the capital shifted to Athens, this royal palace was built to house King Otto and his wife, Queen Amalia. The atmosphere was tense. After fighting so fiercely for its independence from the Ottomans, the Greeks now chafed under royal rule from a dictatorial Bavarian monarch. The palace's over-the-top luxury only angered impoverished locals.

On September 3, 1843, angry rioters gathered in the square to protest, demanding a democratic constitution. King Otto stepped onto the balcony of this building, quieted the mob, and gave them what they wanted. The square was dubbed Syntagma (Constitution), and modern Athens was born. The former royal palace has been the home of the Greek parliament since 1935. Today this is where 300 Greek parliamentarians (elected to four-year terms) tend to the business of the state—or, as more cynical locals would say, become corrupt and busily get themselves set up for their cushy, post-political lives.

▶ *Cross back to the heart of Syntagma Square, and focus on the grand building fronting its north side.*

Parliament overlooking Syntagma Square.   Neoclassical Hotel Grande Bretagne.

❹ Hotel Grande Bretagne and Neoclassical Syntagma

Imagine the original Syntagma Square (which was on the outskirts of town in the early 19th century): a big front yard for the new royal palace, with the country's influential families building mansions around it. Surviving examples include Hotel Grande Bretagne, the adjacent Hotel King George Palace, the Zappeion in the National Garden (not visible from here), and the stately architecture lining Vasilissis Sofias avenue behind the palace (now embassies and museums).

These grand buildings date from Athens' Otto-driven Neoclassical makeover. Eager to create a worthy capital for Greece, Otto imported teams of Bavarian architects to draft a plan of broad avenues and grand buildings in what they imagined to be the classical style. This "Neoclassical" look is symmetrical and geometrical, with pastel-colored buildings highlighted in white trim. The windows are rectangular, flanked by white Greek half-columns (pilasters), fronted by balconies, and topped with cornices. Many of the buildings themselves are also framed at the top with cornices. When you continue on this walk, notice not only the many Neoclassical buildings, but also the more modern buildings that try to match the same geometric lines.

Syntagma Square is also worth a footnote in American Cold War history. In December of 1944, Greek communists demonstrated here, inducing the US to come to the aid of the Greek government. This became the basis (in 1947) for the Truman Doctrine, which pledged US aid to countries fighting communism and helped shape American foreign policy for the next 50 years.

▶ *Head down to the bottom of Syntagma (directly across from the Parliament). Stroll down the traffic-free street near the McDonald's.*

⑤ Ermou Street

The pedestrian mall called Ermou (AIR-moo) leads from Syntagma down through the Plaka to Monastiraki, then continues westward to the ancient Keramikos Cemetery and the Gazi district. Not long ago, this street epitomized all that was terrible about Athens: lousy building codes, tacky neon signs, double-parked trucks, and noisy traffic. When Ermou was first pedestrianized in 2000, merchants were upset. Now they love the ambience created as countless locals stroll through what has become a people-friendly shopping zone.

This has traditionally been the street of women's shops. However, these days Ermou is dominated by high-class international chain stores, which appeal to young Athenians but turn off older natives, who lament the lack of local flavor. For authentic, hole-in-the-wall shopping, many Athenians prefer the streets just to the north, such as Perikleous, Lekka, and Kolokotroni (for shopping tips, see the Practicalities chapter).

Even so, this people-crammed boulevard is a pleasant place for a wander. Do just that, proceeding gradually downhill and straight ahead for seven blocks. As you window-shop, notice that many of Ermou's department stores are housed in impressive Neoclassical mansions. Talented street performers (many of them former music professionals from Eastern Europe) provide an entertaining soundtrack. All of Athens walks along here, from businesspeople to Orthodox priests. Keep an eye out for vendors selling various snacks—including pretzel-like sesame rings called *koulouri* and slices of fresh coconut.

After six short blocks, on the right (at the intersection with Evangelistrias/Ευαγγελιστριασ), look for the little **book wagon** selling cheap lit. You'll likely see colorful, old-fashioned alphabet books (labeled ΑΛΦΑΒΗΤΑΡΙΟ, *Alphabetario*), which have been reprinted for nostalgic older Greeks. Remember that the English word "alphabet" comes from the first two Greek letters (alpha, beta).

You'll reach a little church in the middle of the street (we'll visit it next, in Part 2 of this walk). Cap this first part of your walk (20 yards past the little church) by popping into the **shopping mall** on the right at Ermou 54. Enjoy the cool air along with the cool architecture. This slice of 19th-century Athenian elegance has been nicely preserved and earns its keep today as a place to shop.

PART 2: THE GREEK ORTHODOX CHURCH

In the fourth century A.D., the Roman Empire split in half, dividing Eastern Europe and the Balkan Peninsula down the middle. Seven centuries later, with the Great Schism, the Christian faith diverged along similar lines, into two separate branches: Roman Catholicism in the west (based in Rome) and Eastern or Byzantine Orthodoxy in the east (based in Constantinople—today's Istanbul). Rather than having one centralized headquarters (such as the Vatican for Catholicism), the Eastern Orthodox Church is divided into about a dozen regional branches (such as the Russian Orthodox Church and the Greek Orthodox Church), each remaining administratively independent. This part of our walk introduces you to the Orthodox faith of Greece, including stops at three churches.

▶ *Stranded in the middle of both Ermou street and the commercial bustle of the 21st century is a little medieval church.*

❻ Church of Kapnikarea

After the ancient Golden Age, but before Otto and the Ottomans, Athens was part of the Byzantine Empire (A.D. 323-1453). In the 11th and 12th centuries, Athens boomed, and several Eastern Orthodox churches like this one were constructed.

The Church of Kapnikarea—named for the tax on the cloth merchants that once lined this square—is a classic 11th-century Byzantine church. Notice that Kapnikarea is square and topped with a central dome. Telltale signs of a Byzantine church include tall arches over the windows, stones surrounded by a frame of brick and mortar, and a domed cupola with a cross on top. The large white blocks are scavenged from other, earlier monuments (also typical of Byzantine churches from this era). Over the door is a mosaic of glass and gold leaf, which, though modern, is made in the traditional Byzantine style.

If the church is open, step inside. (If it's closed, don't fret—we'll be visiting a couple of similar churches later.) The church has no nave, just an entrance hall. Notice the symmetrical Greek-cross floor plan. It's decorated with standing candelabras, hanging lamps, tall arches, a wooden pulpit, and a few chairs. If you wish, you can do as the Greeks do and follow the standard candle-buying, icon-kissing ritual (see sidebar on page 26). The icon displayed closest to the door gets changed with the church

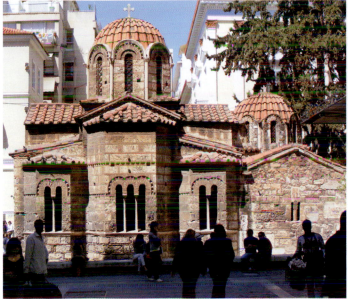

Church of Kapnikarea—"icon"-ic Orthodox in the middle of trendy Ermou street.

calendar. You may notice lipstick smudges on the protective glass and a candle-recycling box behind the candelabra.

Look up into the central dome, lit with windows, which symbol-izes heaven. Looking back down is the face of Jesus, the omnipotent *Pantocrator* God blessing us on Earth. He holds a Bible in one hand and blesses us with the other. On the walls are iconic murals of saints. Notice the focus on the eyes, which are considered a mirror of the soul and a symbol of its purity.

▶ *When you leave the church, turn south toward the Acropolis and proceed downhill on Kapnikareas street. Up ahead, catch a glimpse of the Acropolis. Go two blocks, to the traffic-free Pandrossou shopping street. Turn left and walk (passing the recommended Restaurant Hermion) up the pedestrian street to the cathedral.*

Rituals of the Eastern Orthodox Church

While the doctrine of Catholic and Orthodox churches remains very similar, many of the rituals are different. As you enter any Greek Orthodox church, you can join in the standard routine: Drop a coin in the wooden box, pick up a candle, say a prayer, light the candle, and place it in the candelabra. Make the sign of the cross and kiss the icon.

Worshippers stand through the service as a sign of respect (though some older parishioners sit on the seats along the walls). Traditionally, women stand on the left side, men on the right (but are an equal distance from the altar—to represent that all are equal before God). Orthodox services generally involve chanting (a dialogue that goes back and forth between the priest and the congregation), and the church is filled with the evocative aroma of incense, combining to heighten the experience for the worshippers. Each of these elements does its part to help the worshipper transcend the physical world and enter communion with the spiritual one.

As you visit Athens' churches, look for the following objects:

Iconostasis: An altar screen covered with curtains and icons divides the lay community from the priests—the material world from the spiritual one.

Cross: The Orthodox faith tends to use a Greek cross, with four equal arms (like a plus sign, sometimes inside a circle), which focuses on God's perfection (as opposed to the longer Latin cross, which more literally evokes the Crucifixion).

Icons: Unlike many Catholic church decorations, Orthodox icons (golden paintings of saints) are not intended to be lifelike. Packed with intricate symbolism and cast against a shimmering golden background, they're meant to remind viewers of the metaphysical nature of Jesus and the saints rather than their physical form, which is considered irrelevant.

Christ as *Pantocrator:* This image, so familiar to Orthodox Christians, shows Christ as King of the Universe, facing directly out, with penetrating eyes. Behind him is a halo divided by a cross, with only three visible arms—an Orthodox symbol for the Trinity (the fourth arm is hidden behind Christ).

❼ Cathedral (Mitropolis) and Cathedral Square (Plateia Mitropoleos)

Built in 1842, this "metropolitan church" (as the Greek Orthodox call their cathedrals) is the most important in Athens, which makes it the head church of the Greek Orthodox faith. Unfortunately, it's unremarkable and oddly ramshackle inside and out...and has been decorated by scaffolding since the earthquake of 1989.

If it's open, head inside. Looking up (likely through more scaffolding), you'll notice balconies. Traditionally, women worshipped apart from men in the balconies upstairs. Women got the vote in Greece in 1954, and since about that time, they've been able to worship in the prime, ground-floor real estate alongside the men.

When you're back outside on the square, notice the statue facing the cathedral. This was erected by Athens' Jewish community as thanks to **Archbishop Damaskinos** (1891-1949), the rare Christian leader who stood up to the Nazis during the occupation of Greece. At great personal risk, Damaskinos formally spoke out against the Nazi occupiers on behalf of the Greek Jews he saw being deported to concentration camps. When a Nazi commander threatened to put Damaskinos before a firing squad, the archbishop defiantly countered that he should be hanged instead, in good Orthodox tradition. After the occupation, Damaskinos served as regent and then prime minister of Greece until the king returned from exile.

Here Damaskinos is depicted wearing the distinctive hat of an archbishop (a kind of fez with cloth hanging down the sides). He carries a staff and blesses with his right hand, making a traditional Orthodox sign of the cross, touching his thumb to his ring finger. This gesture forms the letters

Orthodox cathedral, with scaffolding.

Archbishop making the sign of Jesus.

ICXC, the first and last letters of the Greek name for Jesus Christ (ΙΗΣΟΥΣ ΧΡΙΣΤΟΣ—traditionally C was substituted for Σ). Make the gesture yourself with your right hand. Touch the tip of your thumb to the tip of your ring finger and check it out: Your pinkie forms the I, your slightly crossed index and middle fingers are the X, and your thumb and ring finger make a double-C. Jesus Christ, that's clever. If you were a priest, you'd make the sign of the cross three times, to symbolize the Father, the Son, and the Holy Spirit.

The double-headed eagle that hangs around Damaskinos' neck is an important symbol of the Orthodox faith. It evokes the Byzantine Empire, during which Orthodox Christianity was at its peak as the state religion. Appropriately, the eagle's twin heads have a double meaning: The Byzantine Emperor was both the secular and spiritual leader of his realm, which exerted its influence over both East and West. (Coincidentally, a similar symbol has been used by many other kingdoms and empires, including the Holy Roman Empire and the Austro-Hungarian Empire.)

At the far end of the square from the cathedral is another statue, of a warrior holding a sword. This is **Emperor Constantine XI Palaeologus** (1404-1453), the final ruler of the Byzantine Empire. He was killed defending Constantinople from the invading Ottomans, led by Mehmet the Conqueror. Considered the "last Greek king" and an unofficial saint, Constantine XI's death marked the ascension of the Ottomans as overlords of the Greeks for nearly four centuries. On his boots and above his head, you'll see the double-headed eagle again.

▶ *The small church tucked behind the right side of the cathedral is the...*

Constantine XI couldn't stop the Ottomans.

Agios Eleftherios church, with old stones.

❽ Church of Agios Eleftherios

A favorite of local church connoisseurs, the 13th-century Church of Agios Eleftherios (St. Eleutherius) is sometimes referred to as "the old cathedral" and was used by the archbishops of Athens after the Ottomans evicted them from the church within the Parthenon. It's a jigsaw-puzzle hodge-podge of B.C. and A.D. adornments (and even tombstones) from earlier buildings. For example, the carved marble reliefs above the door were scavenged from the Ancient Agora in the 12th century. They are part of a calendar of second century ancient Athenian festivals. The frieze running along the top of the building depicts a B.C. procession.

Later, Christians added their own symbols to the same panels—making the church a treasure trove of medieval symbolism. There are different kinds of crosses (Maltese, Latin, double) as well as carved rosettes, stars, flowers, and griffins feeding on plants and snakes. Walk around the entire exterior. Then, step inside to sample 12th-century Orthodox simplicity.

▶ *Exit the church, go around its right side, then turn right. Look for a street sign that reads* ΑΓΙΑΣ ΦΙΛΟΘΕΗΣ, *and start up...*

❾ Agia Filotheis Street

This neighborhood is a hive of activity for Orthodox clerics. The priests dress all in black, wear beards, and don those fez-like hats. Despite their hermetic look, most priests are husbands, fathers, and well-educated pillars of the community, serving as counselors and spiritual guides to Athens' cosmopolitan populace.

Notice the many **religious objects stores**—such as Theodoro-poulos—that line the street (most are open Mon, Wed, and Fri 8:30-15:00; Tue and Thu 8:30-14:00 & 17:30-20:30; closed Sat-Sun). Cross the busy Apollonos street and continue exploring the shops of Agia Filotheis street. The Orthodox religion comes with ample paraphernalia: icons, gold candelabras, hanging lamps, incense burners, oil lamps, chalices, various crosses, and gold objects worked in elaborate repoussé design. Pop into the **stoas** (arcades) at #15 and #17 (on the left) to see workshops of artisans who make these objects—painters creating or restoring icons, tailors making bishops' hats and robes, carvers making devotional statuettes.

A few more steps up on the left, the ❿ **Church of Agia Filotheis** and an office building (at #19) that serves as the headquarters for the Greek Orthodox Church. Athenians come here to file the paperwork to make their marriages (and divorces) official.

PART 3: ATHENS' "OLD TOWN" (THE PLAKA AND ANAFIOTIKA)

This part of our walk explores the atmospheric, twisty lanes of old Athens. Remember, back before Athens became Greece's capital in the early 1800s, the city was a small town consisting of little more than what we'll see here.

▶ *Continue up Agia Filotheis street until you reach a tight five-way intersection. The street that runs ahead and to your right (labeled ΑΔΡΙΑΝΟΥ)—choked with souvenir stands and tourists—is our next destination. Look uphill and downhill along...*

⑪ Adrianou Street

This intersection may be the geographical (if not atmospheric) center of the neighborhood called the Plaka. Touristy Adrianou street is a main pedestrian drag that cuts through the Plaka, running roughly east-west from Monastiraki to here. Adrianou offers the full gauntlet of Greek souvenirs: worry beads, sea sponges, olive products, icons, carpets, jewelry, sandals, faux vases and Greek statues, profane and tacky T-shirts, and on and on. It also offers plenty of cafés for tourists seeking a place to sit and rest their weary feet.

▶ *Bear left onto Adrianou and walk uphill several blocks, following it as it curves to the right (south). Finally, the street dead-ends at a T-intersection with Lysikratous street. (There's a small square ahead on the left, with palm trees, the Byzantine church of Agia Aikaterini, and an excavated area showing the street level 2,000 years ago.)*

From here, you can turn right and take a few steps uphill to the Lysicrates Monument and Square (and skip ahead to the section on the Lysicrates Monument). But if you've got more time and stamina, it's worth a two-block walk to the left down Lysikratous street to reach the remains of the Arch of Hadrian.

⑫ Hadrianopolis: Arch of Hadrian and Temple of Olympian Zeus

After the Romans conquered the Greeks, Roman emperor Hadrian (or Adrianou) became a major benefactor of the city of Athens. He built a triumphal arch, completed a temple beyond it (now ruined), and founded a library we'll see later. The area beyond the arch was known as Hadrianopolis, a planned neighborhood built by the emperor. The grand

Adrianou—the Plaka's touristy main drag.

Hadrian's arch marks the Roman conquest.

archway overlooks the bustling, modern Vasilissis Amalias avenue, facing the Plaka and Acropolis. (If you turned left and followed this road for 10 minutes, you'd pass the TI, then end up back on Syntagma Square—where we began this walk.)

Arch of Hadrian

The arch's once-brilliant-white Pentelic marble is stained by the exhaust fumes from some of Athens' worst traffic. The arch is topped with Corinthian columns, the Greek style preferred by the Romans. Hadrian built it in A.D. 132 to celebrate the completion of the Temple of Olympian Zeus (which lies just beyond—described next). Like a big *paifang* gate marking the entrance to a modern Chinatown, this arch represented the dividing line between the ancient city and Hadrian's new "Roman" city. An inscription on the west side informs the reader, "This is Athens, ancient city of Theseus," while the opposite frieze carries the message, "This is the city of Hadrian, and not of Theseus." This must have been a big deal for Hadrian, as the emperor himself came here to celebrate the inauguration.

► *Look past the arch to see the huge (and I mean huge) Corinthian columns remaining from what was once a temple dedicated to the Olympian Zeus. For a closer look, cross the busy boulevard (crosswalk to the right). You can pretty much get the gist by looking through the fence. But if you want to get close to those giant columns and wander the ruins, enter the site (covered by Acropolis ticket). To reach the entrance (a five-minute walk), curl around the left side of the arch, then turn right (following the fence) up the intersecting street called Vasilissis Olgas. The entrance to the temple is a few minutes' walk up, on the right-hand side.*

Temple of Olympian Zeus (Olympieion)

This largest temple in ancient Greece took almost 700 years to finish. It was begun late in the sixth century B.C. during the rule of the tyrant Peisistratos. But the task proved beyond him. The temple lay abandoned—half-built— for centuries, until the Roman emperor Hadrian arrived to finish the job in A.D. 131. When completed, it was 360 feet by 145 feet, consisting of 2 rows of 20 columns on each of the long sides and 3 rows of 8 columns along each end. Although only 15 of the original 104 Corinthian columns remain standing, their sheer size (a towering 56 feet high) is enough to create a powerful impression of the temple's scale. The fallen column—which resembles a tipped-over stack of bottle caps—was toppled by a storm in 1852. The temple once housed a suitably oversized statue of Zeus, head of the Greek gods who lived on Mount Olympus, and an equally colossal statue of Hadrian.

▶ *Return to Lysikratous street and backtrack two blocks, continuing past the small square with the church you passed earlier. After another block, you'll run into another small, leafy square with the Acropolis rising behind it. In the square is an elegant, round, white-columned monument.*

⑬ Lysicrates Monument and Square

This elegant marble monument has Corinthian columns that support a dome with a (damaged) statue on top. A frieze runs along the top, representing Dionysus turning pirates into dolphins. The monument is the sole survivor of many such monuments that once lined this ancient "Street of the Tripods." It was so called because the monuments came with bronze tripods that displayed grand ornamental pottery vases and cauldrons (like those you'll see in the museums) as trophies. These ancient "Oscars" were awarded to winners of choral and theatrical competitions staged at the Theater of Dionysus on the southern side of the Acropolis. This now-lonely monument was erected in 334 B.C. by "Lysicrates of Kykyna, son of Lysitheides"—proud sponsor of the winning choral team that year. Excavations around the monument have uncovered the foundations of other monuments, which are now reburied under a layer of red sand and awaiting further study.

The square itself, shaded by trees, is a pleasant place to take a break before climbing the hill. Have a frappé or coffee at the café tables (€3.50), grab a cheap cold drink from the cooler in the hole-in-the-wall grocery store to the left, or just sit for free on the benches under the trees.

At the Temple of Olympian Zeus, the Romans used Greek styles to build on a colossal scale.

Lysicrates Monument—an ancient "Oscar."

Lykavittos Hill, seen from the Acropolis.

► *Passing the monument on its left-hand side, head uphill toward the Acropolis, climbing the staircase called Epimenidou street. At the top of the stairs, turn right onto Stratonos street, which leads around the base of the Acropolis. As you walk along, the Acropolis and a row of olive trees are on your left. The sound of the crickets evokes for Athenians the black-and-white movies that were filmed in this area in the 1950s and '60s. To your right, you'll catch glimpses of another hill off in the distance.*

⑭ View of Lykavittos Hill

This cone-shaped hill (sometimes spelled "Lycabettus") topped with a tiny white church is the highest in Athens, at just over 900 feet above sea level. The hill can be reached by a funicular, which leads up from the Kolonaki neighborhood to a restaurant and view terrace at the top. Although it looms high over the cityscape, Lykavittos Hill will always be overshadowed by the hill you're climbing now.

► *At the small Church of St. George of the Rock (Agios Georgios), go uphill, along the left fork. As you immerse yourself in a maze of tiny, whitewashed houses, follow signs that point to the Acropolis (even if the path seems impossibly narrow). This charming "village" is a neighborhood called...*

⑮ Anafiotika

These lanes and homes were built by people from the tiny Cycladic island of Anafi, who came to Athens looking for work after Greece gained its independence from the Ottomans. In this delightful spot, nestled beneath the walls of the Acropolis, the big city seems miles away. Keep following the

Acropolis signs as you weave through narrow paths, lined with flowers and dotted with cats dozing peacefully in the sunshine (or slithering luxuriously past your legs). Though ancestors of the original islanders still live here, Anafiotika (literally "little Anafi") is slowly becoming a place for wealthy locals to keep an "island cottage" in the city. Posters of Anafi hang here and there, evoking the sandy beaches of the ancestral home island.

▶ *You'll know you're on the right track when you see a religious building with the date 1874 on a wall plaque. Follow the narrow walkway a few more steps. Emerging from the maze of houses, you'll hit a fork at a wider, cobbled lane. Turn right (downhill) and continue down the steep incline. When you hit a wider road (Theorias), turn left and walk toward the small, Byzantine-style Church of the Metamorphosis. (Note: To walk to the Acropolis entry from here, continue along this road as it bends left around the hill.) Just before this church, turn right and go down the steep, narrow staircase (a lane called Klepsydras, labeled ΚΛΕΨΥΔΡΑΣ).*

The whitewashed settlement of Anafiotika, on the Acropolis, preserves a village ambience.

Cross the street called Tholou and continue down Klepsydras. The lane gets even narrower (yes, keep going between the plants). Eventually you'll run into a railing overlooking some ruins.

16 The Roman Forum and the Tower of the Winds

The rows of columns framing this rectangular former piazza were built by the Romans, who conquered Greece around 150 B.C. and stayed for centuries. This square—sometimes called the "Roman Agora"—was the commercial center, or forum, of Roman Athens, with a colonnade providing shade for shoppers browsing the many stores that fronted it. Centuries later, the Ottomans made this their grand bazaar. The mosque survives (although its minaret, like all minarets in town, was torn down by the Greeks when they won their independence from the Ottomans in the 19th century).

Take a few steps to the right to see the octagonal, domed **Tower of the Winds** (a.k.a. "Bath-House of the Winds"). The carved reliefs depict winds as winged humans who fly in, bringing the weather. Built in the first century B.C., this building was an ingenious combination of clock, weathervane, and guide to the planets. The beautifully carved reliefs are believed to represent the ancient Greek symbols for the eight winds. Even local guides don't know which is which, but the reliefs are still beautiful.

As you walk down the hill (curving right, then left around the fence, always going downhill), you'll see reliefs depicting a boy with a harp, a boy with a basket of flowers (summer wind), a relief with a circle, and a guy blowing a conch shell—he's imitating Boreas, the howling winter wind from the north. The tower was once capped with a weathervane in the form of a bronze Triton (half-man, half-fish) that spun to indicate which wind was blessing or cursing the city at the moment. Bronze rods (no longer visible) protruded from the walls and acted as sundials to indicate the time. And when the sun wasn't shining, people told time using the tower's sophisticated water clock, powered by water piped in from springs on the Acropolis. Much later, under Ottoman rule, dervishes used the tower as a place for their whirling worship and prayer.

▶ *It's possible but unnecessary to enter the ruins: You've seen just about everything from this vantage point. If you do decide to enter the ruins, follow the spike-topped fence below the tower down Pelopida street and through an outdoor dining zone (where it curves and becomes Epameinonda) to reach the ticket office and entry gate, near the tallest*

Roman Forum, heart of Roman Athens.

Tower of the Winds, with carved reliefs.

standing colonnade (tower explained on a plaque inside; entry covered by Acropolis ticket). Don't confuse the Roman Forum with the older, more interesting Ancient Agora, which is near the end of this walk.

Otherwise, from just below the Tower of the Winds, head down Aiolou street to...

🟠 Agora Square (Plateia Agoras)

This leafy, restaurant-filled square is the touristy epicenter of the Plaka. A handy Internet café is nearby (Bits and Bytes, just off Agora Square at Kapnikareas 19), as well as a stop for one of the city's tourist trains (see page 171).

On the left side of the square, you'll see the second-century A.D. ruins of the 🔵 **Library of Hadrian.** Four lone columns sit atop the apse-like foundations of what was once a cultural center (library, lecture halls, garden, and art gallery), built by the Greek-loving Roman emperor for the Athenian citizens.

▶ *Continue downhill alongside the ruins to the next block, where Aiolou intersects with the claustrophobic Pandrossou market street (which we walked along earlier). This crowded lane is worked by expert pickpockets—be careful. Look to the right up Pandrossou: You may see merchants sitting in folding chairs with their backs to each other, competition having soured their personal relationships. Turn left on Pandrossou and wade through the knee-deep tacky tourist souvenirs. The second shop is dedicated to "The Round Goddess"—soccer. ("Soccer widows" are as prevalent in Greece as "football widows" in the US.) Continue until you spill out into Monastiraki Square.*

⑲ Monastiraki Square

We've made it from Syntagma Square—the center of urban Athens—to the city's *other* main square, Monastiraki Square, the gateway to the touristy Old Town. To get oriented to Monastiraki Square, stand in the center, face the small church with the cross on top (which is north), and pan clockwise.

→ **Self-Guided Spin-Tour:** The name Monastiraki means "Little Monastery." It refers to this square, the surrounding neighborhood, the flea-market action nearby...and the cute **Church of the Virgin** in the square's center (12th-century Byzantine, mostly restored with a much more modern bell tower).

Beyond that (straight ahead from the end of the square), **Athinas street** heads north to the Central Market, Omonia Square, and (after about a mile) the National Archaeological Museum.

Just to the right (behind the little church) is the head of **Ermou street**—the bustling shopping drag we walked down earlier (though no longer traffic-free here). If you turned right and walked straight up Ermou, you'd be back at Syntagma Square in 10 minutes.

Next (on the right, in front of the little church) comes Mitropoleos street—Athens' ⑳ **"Souvlaki Row."** Clogged with outdoor tables, this atmospheric lane is home to a string of restaurants that serve sausage-shaped, skewered meat—grilled up spicy and tasty. The place on the corner—Bairaktaris (ΜΠΑΪΡΑΚΤΑΡΗΣ)—is the best known, its walls lined with photos of famous politicians and artists who come here for souvlaki and pose with the owner. But the other two joints along here—Thanasis and Savas—have a better reputation for their souvlaki. You can sit at the tables, or, for a really cheap meal, order a souvlaki to go for less than €2

Leafy Agora Square, lined with eateries.

Monastiraki Square—a transportation hub.

(see listings in the Eating chapter.) A few blocks farther down Mitropoleos is the cathedral we visited earlier.

Continue spinning clockwise. Just past Pandrossou street (where you entered the square), you'll see a **㉑ former mosque** (look for the Arabic script under the portico and over the wooden door). Known as the Tzami (from the Turkish word for "mosque"), this was a place of worship from the 15th to 19th centuries. Today, it houses the Museum of Greek Folk Art's **ceramics collection.** The mosque's front balcony (no ticket required) offers fine views over Monastiraki Square.

To the right of the mosque, behind the fence along Areos street, you might glimpse some huge Corinthian columns. This is the opposite end of the **Library of Hadrian** complex we saw earlier. Areos street stretches up toward the Acropolis. If you were to walk a block up this street, then turn right on Adrianou, you'd reach the **㉒ Ancient Agora**—one of Athens' top ancient attractions. Beyond the Agora are the delightful Thissio neighborhood, ancient Keramikos Cemetery, and Gazi district.

As you continue panning clockwise, next comes the pretty yellow building that houses the **Monastiraki Metro station.** This was Athens' original, British-built, 19th-century train station—Neoclassical with a dash of Byzantium. This bustling Metro stop is the intersection of two lines: the old line 1 (green, with connections to the port of Piraeus, the Thissio neighborhood, and Victoria—near the National Archaeological Museum) and the modern line 3 (blue, with connections to Syntagma Square and the airport). The stands in front of the station sell seasonal fruit and are popular with commuters.

Just past the station, Ifestou street leads downhill into the **㉓ flea market** (antiques, jewelry, cheap clothing, and so on—daily, best on Sun 8:00-15:00). If locals need a screw for an old lamp, they know they'll find it here.

Keep panning clockwise. Just beyond busy Ermou street (to the left of Athinas street) is the happening **Psyrri** district. For years a run-down slum, this zone is being gentrified by twentysomethings with a grungy sense of style. Packed with cutting-edge bars, restaurants, cafés, and nightclubs, it may seem foreboding and ramshackle, but is actually fun to explore.

㉔ Monastiraki Metro Station

Finish your walk by stepping into the Monastiraki Metro station and riding the escalator down to see an exposed bit of ancient Athens. Excavations for the Metro revealed an ancient aqueduct, which confined Athens' Eridanos River to a canal. The river had been a main axis of the town since the eighth century B.C. In the second century A.D., Hadrian and his engineers put a roof over it, turning it into a more efficient sewer. You're looking at Roman brick and classic Roman engineering. A cool mural shows the treasure trove archaeologists uncovered with the excavations.

This walk has taken us from ancient ruins to the Roman era, from medieval churches and mosques to the guerrilla fighters of Greek Independence, through the bustling bric-a-brac of the modern city, and finally to a place where Athens' infrastructure—both ancient and modern—mingles.

▶ *Our walk is over. If you're ready for a break, savor a spicy souvlaki on "Souvlaki Row."*

Flea market chairs, for a well-deserved rest.

Acropolis Tour

Ακρόπολη

Rising above the sprawl of Athens, the Acropolis ("high city") is a lasting testament to the glory of Greece's Golden Age. Even now, it's hard to overstate the historic and artistic importance of this place.

Its four major monuments—the Parthenon, Erechtheion, Propylaea, and Temple of Athena Nike—have survived remarkably well given the beating they've taken over the centuries. While the Persians, Ottomans, and Lord Elgin were cruel to the Acropolis in the past, it's now battling acid rain and pollution. Ongoing restoration means that you might see some scaffolding—but even that can't detract from the greatness of this sight.

Climbing Acropolis Hill and rambling its ruins, you'll feel like you've journeyed back in time to the birthplace of Western civilization itself.

ORIENTATION

Cost: €12 for Acropolis ticket (also covers Athens' other major ancient sights—see page 123); free for kids 18 and under, on Sun Nov-March, and on national holidays.

Hours: Daily May-mid-Sept 8:00-20:00, mid-Sept-Oct until 18:00, Nov-April until 17:00, last entry 30 minutes before closing.

When to Go: Get there early or late to avoid the crowds and midday heat. The place is miserably packed with tour groups from 10:00 to about 12:30 (when you might have to wait up to 45 minutes to get inside). On some days, as many as 6,000 cruise passengers converge on the Acropolis in a single morning. It's not the ticket-buying line that holds you up; instead, the worst lines are caused by the bottleneck of people trying to squeeze into the site through the Propylaea gate (so buying your ticket elsewhere doesn't ensure a speedy entry). Late in the day, as the sun goes down, the white Parthenon stone gleams a creamy golden brown, and what had been a tourist war zone is suddenly peaceful. On my last visit, I showed up late and had the place to myself in the cool of early evening.

Getting There: There's no way to reach the Acropolis without a lot of climbing (though people with disabilities can use an elevator). Figure a 10- to 20-minute hike from the base of the Acropolis up to the hilltop archaeological site. There are multiple paths up to the Acropolis, but the only ticket office and site entrance are at the western end of the hill (to the right as you face the Acropolis from the Plaka).

If you're touring the Ancient Agora, you can hike directly up to the Acropolis entrance along the Panathenaic Way. The approach from the Dionysiou Areopagitou pedestrian zone behind (south of) the Acropolis is a bit less steep. From this walkway, various well-marked paths funnel visitors up to the entrance; the least steep one climbs up from the parking lot at the western end of the pedestrian zone. You can reach this path either by taxi or by tourist train (the Athens Happy Train—see page 171), but note that it still involves quite a bit of uphill hiking.

If you use a wheelchair, you can take the elevator that ascends the Acropolis (from the ticket booth, go around the left side of the hilltop). However, once up top, the site is not particularly level or

well-paved, so you may need help navigating the steep inclines and uneven terrain.

Information: Supplement this tour with the free information brochure (you may have to ask for it when you buy your ticket) and info plaques posted throughout; tel. 210-321-4172, www.culture.gr.

Tours: At the entrance, you can hire your own **tour guide,** generally a professional archaeologist (around €90). Or download a **free audio version** of my tour for your mobile device via www.ricksteves.com /audioeurope, iTunes, or the Rick Steves Audio Europe smartphone app. The Acropolis is particularly suited to an audio tour, as it allows your eyes to enjoy the wonders of this sight while your ears learn its story.

Length of This Tour: Allow two hours.

Baggage Check: Backpacks are allowed. Baby strollers are not. There's a checkroom just below the ticket booth near Mars Hill.

Services: There are WCs at the Acropolis ticket booth and more WCs and drinking fountains atop the Acropolis, in the former museum building (behind the Parthenon). Picnicking is not allowed on the premises. A post office and museum shop are near the ticket booth. A vending machine sells bottled water (just inside the ticket-check turnstile and to the right, €0.50, coins only).

Plan Ahead: Wear sensible shoes—Acropolis paths are steep and uneven. In summer, it gets very hot on top, so take a hat, sunscreen, sunglasses, and a bottle of water. Inside the turnstiles, there are no services except WCs and drinking fountains; pack whatever else you'll need (little snacks, guidebooks, camera batteries).

Starring: The Parthenon and other monuments from the Golden Age, plus great views of Athens and beyond.

Acropolis Overview

STANDING RUINS
ORIGINAL FOOTPRINT

To Ancient Agora

To Monastiraki

ANAFIOTIKA

Mars Hill

To Plaka

ELEVATOR

ERECHTHEION

BEULÉ GATE

PROPYLAEA

To Plaka

TICKETS, WC & WATER

ACROPOLIS ENTRANCE

TEMPLE OF ATHENA NIKE

PARTHENON

WC

ODEON OF HERODES ATTICUS

THEATER OF DIONYSUS

To Apostolou Pavlou & Thissio

DIONYSIOU AREOPAGITOU

BUS PARKING LOT

Filopappos Hill

MAKRIGIANNI

Akropoli M

100 Meters

100 Yards

KALLISPERI

ACROPOLIS MUSEUM

BACKGROUND

The Acropolis has been the heart of Athens since the beginning of recorded time (Neolithic era, 6800 B.C.). This limestone plateau, faced with sheer, 100-foot cliffs and fed by permanent springs, was a natural fortress. The Mycenaeans (c. 1400 B.C.) ruled the area from their palace on this hilltop, and Athena—the patron goddess of the city—was worshipped here from around 800 B.C. on.

But everything changed in 480 B.C., when Persia invaded Greece for the second time. As the Persians approached, the Athenians evacuated the city, abandoning it to be looted and vandalized. All of the temples atop the Acropolis were burned to the ground. The Athenians fought back at sea, winning an improbable naval victory at the Battle of Salamis. The

The Acropolis' sheer cliffs have made it a natural fortress since the beginning of time.

Persians were driven out of Greece, and Athens found itself suddenly victorious. Cash poured into Athens from the other Greek city-states, which were eager to be allied with the winning side.

By 450 B.C., Athens was at the peak of its power and the treasury was flush with money...but in the city center, the Acropolis still lay empty, a vast blank canvas. Athens' leader at the time, Pericles, was ambitious and farsighted. He funneled Athens' newfound wealth into a massive rebuilding program. Led by the visionary architect/sculptor Pheidias, the Athenians transformed the Acropolis into a complex of supersized, ornate temples worthy of the city's protector, Athena.

The Parthenon, Erechtheion, Propylaea, and Temple of Athena Nike were built as a coherent ensemble (c. 450-400 B.C.). Unlike most ancient sites, which have layer upon layer of ruins from different periods, the Acropolis we see today was started and finished within two generations— a snapshot of the Golden Age set in stone.

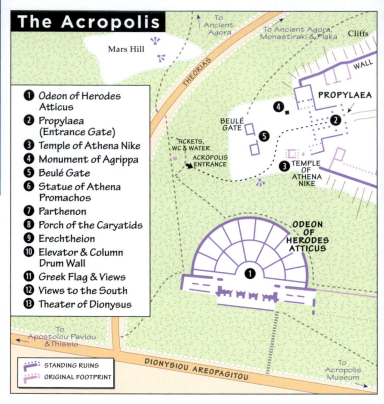

The Acropolis

1. **Odeon of Herodes Atticus**
2. **Propylaea (Entrance Gate)**
3. **Temple of Athena Nike**
4. **Monument of Agrippa**
5. **Beulé Gate**
6. **Statue of Athena Promachos**
7. **Parthenon**
8. **Porch of the Caryatids**
9. **Erechtheion**
10. **Elevator & Column Drum Wall**
11. **Greek Flag & Views**
12. **Views to the South**
13. **Theater of Dionysus**

STANDING RUINS
ORIGINAL FOOTPRINT

THE TOUR BEGINS

▶ *Climb up to the Acropolis ticket booth and the site entrance, located at the west end of the hill.*

Near this entrance (below and toward the Ancient Agora) is the huge, craggy boulder of **Mars Hill** (a.k.a. Areopagus). Consider climbing this rock for great views of the Acropolis' ancient entry gate (the Propylaea, described later) and the Ancient Agora. Mars Hill's bare, polished rock is extremely

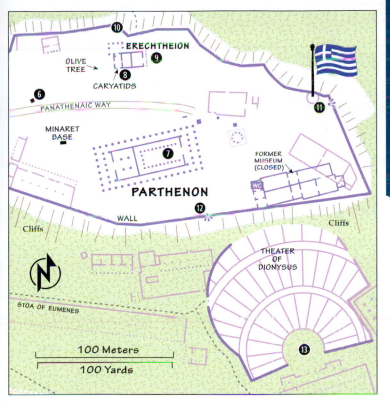

slippery—a metal staircase to the left helps somewhat. (For more on Mars Hill and its role in Christian history, see page 122.)

Before you show your ticket and enter the Acropolis site, make sure you have everything you'll need for your visit. Remember, after you enter the site, there are no services except WCs and water fountains.

► *Enter the site, and start climbing the paths that switchback up the hill, following signs on this one-way tourist route (bearing to the right). Before you reach the summit, peel off to the right for a bird's-eye view of the...*

Propylaea entrance, as seen from Mars Hill.

Odeon theater, for ancients and moderns.

Odeon of Herodes Atticus

This grand venue huddles under the Acropolis' majestic Propylaea entrance gate. While tourists call it a "theater," Greeks know it's technically an *odeon,* as it was mainly used for musical rather than theatrical performances. (*Odeon* comes from the same root as the English "ode," from the Greek word for "song.")

A large 5,000-seat amphitheater built during Roman times, it's still used today for performances. From this perch you get a good look at the stage set-up: a three-quarter-circle orchestra (where musicians and actors performed in Greek-style theater), the overgrown remnants of a raised stage (for actors in the Roman tradition), and an intact stage wall for the backdrop. Originally, it had a wood-and-tile roof as well.

The *odeon* was built in A.D. 161 by Herodes Atticus, a wealthy landowner, in memory of his wife. Herodes Atticus was a Greek with Roman citizenship, a legendary orator, and a friend of Emperor Hadrian. This amphitheater is the most famous of the many impressive buildings he financed around the country.

Destroyed by the invading Herulians a century after it was built, the "Herodion" (as it's also called) was reconstructed in the 1950s to the spectacular state it's still in today. It's open to the public only during performances, such as the annual Athens & Epidavros Festival, which features an international line-up of dance, music, and theater performed beneath the stars. If there's something on tonight, you may see a rehearsal from here. Athenians shudder when visitors—recalling the famous "Yanni Live at the Acropolis" concert—call this stately place "Yanni's Theater."

▶ *After climbing a few steps, you'll see two gates: On the right, steps lead down to the Theater of Dionysus (described on page 124); on the left* is the actual entry uphill into the Acropolis. Stay left and continue up to reach the grand entrance gate of the Acropolis: the Propylaea. Stand at the foot of the (very) steep marble staircase, facing up toward the big Doric columns.

As you face the Propylaea, to your left is a tall, gray stone pedestal with nothing on it: the Monument of Agrippa. On your right, atop the wall, is the Temple of Athena Nike. Behind you stands a doorway in a wall, known as the Beulé Gate.

The Propylaea

The entrance to the Acropolis couldn't be through just any old gate; it had to be the grandest gate ever built. Ancient visitors would stand here, catching their breath before the final push to the summit, and admire these gleaming columns and steep steps that almost fill your entire field of vision. Imagine the psychological impact this awe-inspiring, colonnaded entryway to the sacred rock must have had on ancient Athenians. Unlike today's path, the grand marble staircase didn't zigzag, but instead headed straight up. (A few original stairs survive under the wooden ramp.)

The Propylaea (pro-puh-LEE-ah) is U-shaped, with a large central hallway (the six Doric columns), flanked by side wings that reach out to embrace the visitor. The central building looked like a mini-Parthenon, with Doric columns topped by a triangular pediment. Originally, the Propylaea was painted bright colors and decorated with statues.

The left wing of the Propylaea was the Pinacoteca, or "painting gallery." In ancient times, this space contained artwork and housed visiting dignitaries and VIPs.

The buildings of the Acropolis were all built to complement each

Climbing the Propylaea's staircase.

Temple of Nike, overlooking the Propylaea.

other. The Propylaea, constructed in five short years (437-432 B.C., just after the Parthenon was finished) was designed by Mnesicles, who also did the Erechtheion. The Propylaea gave the visitor a taste of the Parthenon to come. Both buildings are Doric (with Ionic touches) and are aligned east-west, with columns of similar width-to-height ratios.

▶ *Before ascending, notice the monuments flanking the entryway. To the right of the Propylaea, look up high atop the block wall to find the...*

Temple of Athena Nike

The Temple of Athena Nike (Greeks pronounce it "NEEK-ee") was started as the Propylaea was being finished (c. 427-421/415 B.C.). It was designed by Callicrates, one of the architects of the Parthenon. This little temple—nearly square, 11 feet tall, with four columns at both ends—had delightful proportions. Where the Parthenon and Propylaea are sturdy Doric, this temple pioneered the new style of Ionic, with elegant scroll-topped columns.

The Acropolis was mainly dedicated to the goddess Athena, patron of the city. At this temple, she was worshipped for bringing the Athenians victory ("Nike"). A statue of Athena inside the temple celebrated the turning-point victory over the Persians at the Battle of Plataea in 479 B.C. It was also meant to help ensure future victory over the Spartans in the ongoing Peloponnesian War. After the statue's wings were broken by Athenians wanting Athena to stay and protect their city, the place became known as the Temple of Wingless Athena.

The Temple of Athena Nike has undergone extensive restoration. From 2001 to 2010, it was completely disassembled, then cleaned, shored up, and pieced back together. This was the third time in its 2,500-year history that the temple had been entirely taken apart. The Ottomans pulled it down at the end of the 17th century and used the stone elsewhere, but Greeks reassembled the temple after regaining their independence. In 1935, it was taken apart for renovation and put back together in 1939. Unfortunately, that shoddy work did more harm than good—prompting the most recent restoration. Now it's been done the right way and should hold for another 2,500 years.

▶ *To the left (as you face the Propylaea) is the...*

Monument of Agrippa

This 25-foot-high pedestal, made of big blocks of gray marble with yellow veins, reaches as high up as the Temple of Athena Nike. The (now-empty)

The Monument of Agrippa once held grand statues of Athens' heroes and rulers.

pedestal once held a bronze statue of the four-horse chariot driven by the winner of the race at the 178 B.C. Olympics.

Over the centuries, each ruler of Athens wanted to put his mark on the mighty Acropolis. When Rome occupied the city, Marc Antony placed a statue of himself and his girlfriend Cleopatra atop the pedestal. After their defeat, the Roman general Agrippa (son-in-law of Augustus) replaced it with a statue of himself (in 27 B.C.).

▶ *Before entering, look downhill. Behind you is the...*

Beulé Gate

This ceremonial doorway was built by the Romans, who used the rubble from buildings that had recently been destroyed in the barbarian Herulian invasion of A.D. 267. (The gate's French name comes from the archaeologist who discovered it in 1852.) During Roman times, this gate was the official entrance to the Acropolis, making the Propylaea entry even grander.

▶ *Climb the steps (or today's switchback ramps for tourists) and go...*

Inside the Propylaea

Imagine being part of the grand parade of the Panathenaic Festival, held every year (see page 83). The procession started at Athens' city gate (near the Keramikos Cemetery), passed through the Agora, then went around Mars Hill, through the central hall of the Propylaea, and up to the glorious buildings atop the summit of the Acropolis. Ancient Greeks approached the Propylaea by proceeding straight up a ramp in the middle, which narrowed as they ascended, funneling them into the central passageway. There were five doorways into the Propylaea, one between each of the six columns.

Roman-built Beulé Gate.

Stackable column drum, in the Propylaea.

The Propylaea's central hall was once a roofed passageway. The marble-tiled ceiling, now partially restored, was painted sky blue and studded with stars. Floral designs decorated other parts of the building. The interior columns are Ionic, a bit thinner than the Doric columns of the exterior. You'll pass by some big column drums with square holes in the center, where iron pins once held the drums in place. (Greek columns were not usually made from a single piece of stone, but from sections—"column drums"—stacked on top of each other.)

▶ *Pass through the Propylaea. As you emerge out the other end, you're on top of the Acropolis. There it is—the Parthenon! Just like in the books. Stand and take it all in.*

The Acropolis

The "Acropolis rock" is a flat, slightly sloping limestone ridge covering seven acres, scattered with ruins. There's the Parthenon ahead to the right. To the left of that, with the six lady pillars (caryatids), is the Erechtheion. The Panathenaic Way ran between them. The processional street and the buildings were aligned east-west, like the hill.

Ancient visitors here would have come face-to-face with a welcoming 30-foot **Statue of Athena Promachos,** which stood between the Propylaea and the Erechtheion. (Today there's just a field of rubble, with the statue's former location marked by three stones forming a low wall.) This was one of three statues of Athena on the Acropolis. The patron of the city was worshipped for her wisdom, purity, and strength; here she appeared in her role as "Frontline Soldier" *(promachos),* carrying a shield and spear. The statue was cast by Pheidias, the visionary sculptor/architect most responsible for the design of the Acropolis complex. The bronze statue was so tall that the shining tip of Athena's spear was visible from ships at Cape Sounion, 30 miles south. The statue disappeared in ancient times, and no one knows its fate.

Two important buildings, now entirely gone, flanked this statue and the Panathenaic Way. On the right was the Chalkotheke, a practical storage area for the most precious gifts brought to the temple—those made of copper and bronze. On the left stood the Arrephorion, a house where young virgins called *ergastinai* worked at looms to weave the *peplos,* the sacred dress given to Athena on her birthday.

▶ *Move a little closer for the classic view of the...*

Parthenon—The West End

The Parthenon is the hill's showstopper—the finest temple in the ancient world, standing on the highest point of the Acropolis, 490 feet above sea level. The Parthenon is now largely in ruins, partly from the ravages of time, but mostly from a freak accident in 1687, when it suffered bomb damage during a war.

It's impressive enough today, but imagine how awesome the Parthenon must have looked when it was completed nearly 2,500 years ago. This largest Doric temple in Greece is 228 feet long and 101 feet wide. At each end were 8 fluted Doric columns, with 17 columns along each side (46 total), plus 19 inner columns in the Ionic style. The columns are 34 feet high and 6 feet in diameter. In its heyday, the temple was decorated with statues and carved reliefs, all painted in vivid colors. It's considered Greece's greatest Doric temple (though not its purest textbook example because it incorporates Ionic columns and sculpture).

The Parthenon served the cult of Virgin Athena, and functioned as both a temple (with a cult statue inside) and as the treasury of Athens

For 2,000 years, the Parthenon's west end has greeted visitors.

(safeguarding the city's funds, which included the treasury of the Athenian League). You're looking at the west end—the classic view that greets visitors—but the building's main entrance was at the other end.

This large temple was completed in less than a decade (c. 450-440 B.C.), though the sculptural decoration took a few years more (finished c. 432). The project's overall "look" was supervised by the master sculptor-architect Pheidias; built by well-known architects Ictinus and Callicrates; and decorated with carved scenes from Greek mythology by sculptors Agoracritos and Alcamenes.

It's big, sure. But what makes the Parthenon truly exceptional is that the architects used a whole bagful of optical illusions to give the building an ever-so-subtle feeling of balance, strength, and harmonious beauty. Architects know that a long, flat baseline on a building looks to the human eye like it's sagging, and that parallel columns appear to bend away from each other. To create a building that looked harmonious, the Parthenon's ancient architects calculated bends in the construction. The base of the Parthenon actually arches several inches upward in the middle to counteract the "sagging" illusion (and to drain rainwater). Its columns tilt ever so slightly inward (one of the reasons why the Parthenon has withstood earthquakes so well). If you extended all the columns upward several miles, they'd eventually touch. The corner columns are thicker to make them appear the same size as the rest; they're also spaced more closely. And the columns bulge imperceptibly halfway up ("entasis"), giving the subconscious impression of stout, barrel-chested men bearing the weight of the roof. For a building that seems at first to be all about right angles, the Parthenon is amazingly short on straight, structural lines.

All these clever refinements form a powerful subconscious impression on the viewer that brings an otherwise boring architectural box to life. It's amazing to think that all this was planned and implemented in stone so long ago.

The statues and carved reliefs that once decorated the outside of the Parthenon are now mostly fading or missing, but a few remain. Look up at the crossbeam atop the eight columns, decorated with panels of relief carvings called "metopes," depicting Athenians battling Amazons. Originally, there were 92 Doric-style metopes in high relief, mostly designed by Pheidias himself.

The crossbeams once supported a triangular pediment (now gone). This area was once filled in with statues, showing Athena with her olive tree

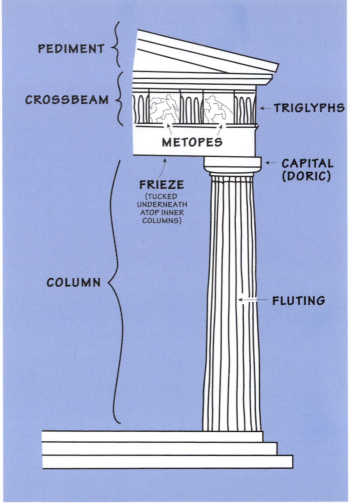

PEDIMENT

CROSSBEAM

TRIGLYPHS

METOPES

CAPITAL (DORIC)

FRIEZE
(TUCKED UNDERNEATH ATOP INNER COLUMNS)

COLUMN

FLUTING

Find the pediment (triangle roofline), metopes (on the crossbeam), and frieze (inner crossbeam).

Metope—carved relief on the crossbeam.

Pediment statues depict Athena's triumph.

competing with Poseidon and his trident to be Athens' patron god. Today just one statue remains (and it's a reconstruction).

Approach closer and look between the eight columns. Inside, there's another row of eight columns, supporting a covered entrance porch. Look up above the inner eight columns. Decorating those crossbeams are more relief carvings—the "frieze." Originally, a 525-foot-long frieze of panels circled the entire building. It showed the Panathenaic parade—dancing girls, men on horseback, sacrificial animals being led to the slaughter—while the gods looked on.

All of these sculptures—metopes, pediment, and frieze—were originally painted in bright colors. Today, most of the originals are in museums across Europe. In the early 1800s, the cream of the crop, the famous "Elgin Marbles," were taken by Lord Elgin to England, where they now sit in the British Museum. The Acropolis Museum (which stands at the base of the hill—you'll see it from a distance later on this tour) was built to house the fragments of the Parthenon sculpture that Athens still owns...and to try to entice the rest back from London.

▶ *Continue along the Panathenaic Way, walking along the long left (north) side of the Parthenon.*

Parthenon—The North Side

This view of the Parthenon gives a glimpse into how the temple was constructed and how it is being reconstructed today by modern archaeologists.

Looking between the columns, you can see remnants of the interior walls, built with thousands of rectangular blocks. The columns formed an open-air porch around the main building, which had an entry hall and *cella* (inner sanctum). Large roof tiles were fitted together atop wooden beams. These tiles were made of ultra-white, translucent Parian marble, and the interior glowed with the light that shone through it.

The Parthenon's columns are in the Doric style—stout, lightly fluted, with no base. The simple capital on top consists of a convex plate topped with a square slab. The capitals alone weigh 12 tons. The crossbeams consist of a lower half ("architrave") and upper half, its metopes interspersed with a pattern of grooves (called triglyphs).

The Parthenon (along with the other Acropolis buildings) was constructed from the very finest materials, including high-quality, white Pentelic marble from Penteliko Mountain, 16 miles away. Unlike the grand structures of the Egyptians (pyramids) and the Romans (Colosseum), the Parthenon was built not by slaves but by free men who drew a salary (though it's possible that slaves worked at the quarries).

Imagine the engineering problems of quarrying and transporting more than 100,000 tons of marble. Most likely, the column drums were cut at the quarry and rolled here. To hoist the drums in place, they used four-poster cranes (and Greek mathematics), centering the drums with a cedar peg in the middle. The drums were held together by metal pins that were coated in lead to prevent corrosion, then fitted into a square hole cut in the center of the drum. (The Ottomans scavenged much of this lead to make bullets, contributing to the destruction of the temple over the ages.) Because the Parthenon's dimensions are not mathematically precise (intentionally so), each piece had to be individually cut and sized to fit its exact place. The Parthenon's stones are so well-crafted that they fit together within a thousandth of an inch. The total cost to build the Parthenon (in today's dollars) has been estimated at over a billion dollars.

Scaffolding and marble on the north side.

Devotees once entered at the east end.

▶ *Continue on to the...*

Parthenon—The East End (Entrance) and Interior

This end was the original entrance to the temple. Over the doorway, the triangular pediment depicted the central event in Athenian history—the Birth of Athena, their patron goddess. Today, the pediment barely survives, and the original statues of the gods are in the British Museum. Originally, the gods were gathered at a banquet (see a copy of the reclining Dionysus at the far left—looking so drunk he's afraid to come down). Zeus got a headache and asked Hephaistos to relieve it. As the other gods looked on in astonishment, Hephaistos split Zeus' head open, and—at the peak of the pediment—out rose Athena. The now-missing statues were surprisingly realistic and three-dimensional, with perfect anatomy and bulging muscles showing through transparent robes.

Imagine this spot during the age of Pericles and Socrates. Stand back far enough to take it all in, mentally replace the 40-foot statue inside, and picture the place in all its glory, on the day of the Panathenaic parade. The parade has traveled through the Agora, ascended the Acropolis, passed through the Propylaea, and arrived here at the entrance of the Parthenon. People gather on the surrounding grass (the hard stone that you see today was once covered with earth and plants). Musicians play flutes and tambourines, girls dance, and men on horseback rein in their restless animals. On open-air altars, the priests offer a sacrifice of 100 oxen (a hecatomb—the ultimate sacrificial gift) to the goddess Athena.

Here at the Parthenon entrance, a select few are chosen to go inside. They proceed up the steps, entering through the majestic columns. First they enter a foyer called the *pronaos,* then continue into the main hall, the *cella*—100 feet long, 60 feet wide, and 4 stories tall. At the far end of the room is an enormous statue of Athena Parthenos ("Athena the Virgin"), standing 40 feet tall. The wooden core of the *chryselephantine* statue (from the Greek *chrysos,* "gold," and *elephantinos,* "ivory") was plated with ivory to represent her skin, and a ton of pure gold (a third of an inch thick) for her garments (or so say local guides). She was dressed as a warrior, wearing a helmet with her shield resting at her side. Her image was reflected in a pool in the center of the room. (The pool also served a practical purpose—the humidity helped preserve the ivory treasures.) In Athena's left hand was a spear propped on the ground. In her upturned right hand was a statuette of Nike—that is, she literally held Victory in the palm of her hand.

The statue was the work of the master Pheidias himself (447-438 B.C.). The statue was carried off to Constantinople in A.D. 426, where it subsequently vanished. A small-scale Roman copy is on display in Athens' National Archaeological Museum (see page 112). Another famous *chryselephantine* statue by Pheidias—of a seated Zeus (originally located in the Temple of Zeus at Olympia)—was considered one of the Seven Wonders of the Ancient World.

The culmination of the Panathenaic parade was the presentation of a newly woven *peplos* to Athena, the patron of the city. Generally, the dress was intended for the life-size wooden statue of Athena kept at the Erechtheion (described later). But during the Grand Panathenaia (every four years), the Athenians presented a huge robe—big enough to cover a basketball court—to the 40-foot Virgin Athena in the Parthenon.

▶ *Behind you, the modern brown-brick building once housed the former Acropolis museum—its collection has been painstakingly moved into the modern Acropolis Museum down the hill. The old museum building may reopen someday as a coffee shop, but for now, it has just WCs and a drinking fountain alongside.*

Across the street from the Parthenon stands the Erechtheion, where the Panathenaic parade ended. There were three entrances to this building: the famous Porch of the Caryatids (the six ladies), the north porch (behind the Erechtheion), and the east end (to the right of the caryatids). Start by enjoying the...

Porch of the Caryatids

An inspired piece of architecture, this balcony has six beautiful maidens functioning as columns that support the roof. Each of the lady-columns has a base beneath her feet, pleated robes as the fluting, and a fruit-basket hat as the capital. Both feminine and functional, they pose gracefully, exposing a hint of leg. It was the first time that the Greeks combined architectural elements and sculpture.

These are faithful copies of the originals, four of which are on display in the Acropolis Museum. The fifth was removed (c. 1805) by the sticky-fingered Lord Elgin, who shipped it to London. The sixth statue is in France. The caryatids were supposedly modeled on *Karyatides*—women from Karyai (modern Karyes, near Sparta on the Peloponnese), famous for their upright posture and noble character.

The Erechtheion was built by Mnesicles (c. 421-406 B.C.), the man

Erechtheion's caryatids—these stone maidens support the roof of this prestigious temple.

who also did the Propylaea. Whereas the Propylaea and Parthenon are both sturdy Doric, the Erechtheion is elegant Ionic. In its day, it was a stunning white building (of Pentelic marble) with black trim and painted columns.

Near the porch (below, to the left) is an olive tree, a replacement for the one Athena planted here in her face-off with Poseidon (described on next page). Olive trees have been called "the gift of Athena to Athens." Greece has more than 100 million of these trees.

▶ *Walk around to the right and view the Erechtheion from the east end, with its six Ionic columns in a row.*

Erechtheion

Though overshadowed by the more impressive Parthenon, the Erechtheion (a.k.a. Erechtheum) was perhaps more prestigious. It stood on one of the oldest sites on the hill, where the Mycenaeans had built their palace. (The huge ruined stones scattered on the south side, facing the Parthenon, are all that's left of the Mycenaean palace.) Inside the Erechtheion was a life-size, olive-wood statue of Athena in her role of Athena Polias ("Protector of the City"). Pericles took the statue with him when the Athenians evacuated their city to avoid the invading Persians. Dating from about 900 B.C., this statue was much older and more venerable than either of Pheidias' colossal statues, supposedly having dropped from the sky as a gift from Athena.

This unique, two-story structure fits nicely into the slope of the hill. The east end (with the six Ionic columns) was the upper-level entrance. The lower entrance was on the north side (on the right), 10 feet lower, where you see six more Ionic columns. (These columns are the "face of the

The Erechtheion sits atop temple ruins.

Erechtheion's Ionic-columned entrance.

Acropolis" that Athenians see from the Plaka.) The Porch of the Caryatids (on the south side of the building, to the left) was yet another entrance. Looking inside the temple, you can make out that the inner worship hall, the *cella,* is divided in two by walls.

This complex layout accommodated the worship of various gods who had been venerated here since the beginning of time. Legend says this was the spot where Athena and Poseidon fought for naming rights to the city. Poseidon threw his trident, which opened a gash in the earth to bring forth water. It left a diagonal crack that you can still see in the pavement of the entrance farthest from the Parthenon (although lightning is a more likely culprit). But Athena won the contest by stabbing a rock with her spear, sprouting an olive tree near the Porch of the Caryatids. The twin *cellas* of the Erechtheion allowed the worship of both gods—Athena and Poseidon—side by side to show that they were still friends.

▶ *Look to the right (beyond the Plaka-facing porch). The modern elevator, useful during the Paralympics in 2004, carries people with disabilities up to the Acropolis. The north wall of the Acropolis has a retaining wall built from column drums. This is about all that remains of an earlier Parthenon that was destroyed after the Persian invasion of 480 B.C. The Persians razed the entire Acropolis, including an unfinished temple then under construction. When the Athenians rebuilt, this column from the old temple helped preserve the bitter memory of the Acropolis' destruction.*

Walk to the far end of the Acropolis. There you'll find an observation platform with a giant...

Greek Flag

The blue-and-white Greek flag's nine stripes symbolize (according to popular myth) the nine syllables of the Greek phrase for "Freedom or Death." That phrase took on new meaning when the Nazis entered Athens in April of 1941. The evzone (elite member of a select infantry unit) who was guarding this flag was ordered by the Nazis to remove it. He calmly took it down, wrapped himself in it...and jumped to his death. About a month later, two heroic teenagers, Manolis Glezos and Apostolis Santas, scaled the wall, took down the Nazi flag, and raised the Greek flag. This was one of the first well-known acts of resistance against the Nazis, and the boys' bravery is honored by a plaque near the base of the steps. To this day, Greeks can see this flag from just about anywhere in Athens and think of their hard-won independence.

After the Golden Age: The Acropolis Through History

Classical: The Parthenon and the rest of the Acropolis' buildings survived through classical times largely intact, despite Herulian looting (A.D. 267). As the Roman Empire declined, precious items were carried off, including the 40-foot Athena statue.

Christian: After nearly a thousand years as Athena's temple, the Parthenon became a Christian church (fifth century A.D.). Pagan sculptures and decorations were removed (or renamed), and the interior was decorated with colorful Christian frescoes. The west end of the building became the main entrance, and the interior was reconfigured with an apse at the east end.

Muslim: In 1456, the Turks arrived and converted the Parthenon into a mosque, adding a minaret. The Propylaea entry gate was used as a palace for the Turkish ruler of Athens. The Turks also used the Parthenon to store gunpowder, unfortunately leading to the greatest catastrophe in the Acropolis' long history.

1687: A Venetian army laid siege to the Acropolis. The Venetians

▶ *Walk out to the end of the rectangular promontory to see the...*

View of Athens

The Ancient Agora spreads below the Acropolis, and the sprawl of modern Athens whitewashes the surrounding hills. In 1830, Athens' population was about 5,000. By 1900, it was 600,000, and during the 1920s, with the influx of Greeks from Turkey, the population surged to 1.5 million. The city's expansion could barely keep up with its exploding population. With the boom times in the 1950s and 1980s, the city grew to nearly four million. Pan around. From this perch, you're looking at the homes of one out of every three Greeks.

Looking down on the **Plaka,** find (looking left to right) the Ancient

didn't care about ancient architecture. As far as they were concerned, it was a lucky hit of mortar fire that triggered the massive explosion that ripped the center out of the Parthenon, rattled the Propylaea and the other buildings, and wiped out the Turkish defenders.

Lord Elgin: In 1801, Lord Elgin, the British Ambassador to the Ottomans in Constantinople, got "permission" from the sultan to gather

sculptures from the Parthenon, buy them from locals, and even saw them off the building. He carted half of them to London. Although a few original frieze, metope, and pediment carvings still adorn the Parthenon, most of the sculptures are on display in museums, including the Acropolis Museum.

From Independence to the Present: In the 19th century, newly independent Greece tore down the Parthenon's minaret and the other post-Classical buildings atop the Acropolis, turning it into an archaeological zone. Since then, the place has been excavated and there have been several renovation efforts.

Agora, with the Temple of Hephaistos. Next comes the Roman Forum (the four columns and palm trees) with its round, white, domed Temple of the Winds monument. The delightful **Anafiotika** neighborhood clings to the Acropolis hillside directly below us (great for a stroll). Beyond that, find the green and red dome of the cathedral.

Lykavittos Hill, Athens' highest point, is crowned with the Chapel of St. George (and an expensive view restaurant; cable car up the hill). Looking farther in the distance, you'll see white bits on the mountains behind—these are the **Pentelic quarries,** the source of the marble used to build (and now restore) the monuments of the Acropolis.

As you continue panning to the right, you'll spot the beige Neoclassical **Parliament** building, marking Syntagma Square; the **National Garden** is

View of Lykavittos Hill.

South view of Temple of Olympian Zeus.

behind and to the right of it. In the garden is the yellow **Zappeion,** an exhibition hall. The green area in the far distance contains the 80,000-seat, marble **Panathenaic Stadium**—an ancient venue (on the site where Golden Age Athens held its games), which was rehabbed in 1896 to help revive the modern Olympics.

▶ *Complete your visual tour of Athens at the south edge of the Acropolis. To reach the viewpoint, walk back toward the Parthenon, then circle along its left side, by the cliff-top wall. Belly up to that wall for a....*

View from the South Side of the Acropolis

Look to the left. In the near distance are the huge columns of the **Temple of Olympian Zeus.** Begun in the sixth century B.C., it wasn't finished until the time of the Roman emperor Hadrian, 700 years later. It was the biggest temple in all of Greece, with 104 Corinthian pillars, housing a 40-foot seated statue of Zeus, a replica of the famous one created by Pheidias in Olympia. This was part of "Hadrianopolis," a planned community in his day, complete with the triumphal **Arch of Hadrian** near the temple.

The **Theater of Dionysus**—which hosted great productions (including works by Sophocles) during the Golden Age—lies in ruins at your feet (covered by your Acropolis ticket).

Beyond the theater is the wonderful **Acropolis Museum,** a black-and-gray modern glass building, with three rectangular floors stacked at irregular angles atop each other. The top floor—which houses replicas and some originals of the Parthenon's art—is angled to match the orientation of that great temple.

Looking right, you see **Filopappos Hill**—the green, tree-dotted hill topped with a marble monument to a popular Roman general in ancient times. This hill is where the Venetians launched the infamous mortar attack of 1687 that destroyed the Parthenon. Today, a theater here hosts popular folk-dancing performances (see page 171).

Farther in the distance, you get a glimpse of the turquoise waters of the **Aegean** (the only island visible is Aegina). While the Persians were burning the Acropolis to the ground, the Athenians watched from their ships as they prepared to defeat them in the history-changing Battle of Salamis. In the distance, far to the right, is the port of Piraeus (the main departure point for boats to the islands).

▶ *Our tour is finished. Enjoy a few final moments with the Acropolis before you leave. If you're not yet ready to return to modern Athens, you can continue your sightseeing at several nearby sights.*

To reach the Theater of Dionysus ruins and the Acropolis Museum: Head left when you exit the Acropolis site, and walk down to the Diony-siou Areopagitou pedestrian boulevard. Turn left and follow this walkway along the base of the Acropolis. First you'll reach the theater entrance (on the left), then the museum (on the right; see the ✪ Acropolis Mu-seum Tour chapter).

To reach the Ancient Agora: Turn right as you exit the Acropolis site, pass Mars Hill, and follow the Panathenaic Way down to the Ancient Agora (possible to enter through the "back door," facing the Acropolis). You'll find the ✪ Ancient Agora Tour in the next chapter.

The odd-angled Acropolis Museum, with the Theater of Dionysus in the foreground.

Ancient Agora Tour

Αρχαία Αγορά

While the Acropolis was the ceremonial showpiece, it was the Agora that was the real heart of ancient Athens. For some 800 years, from its founding in the sixth century B.C. to its destruction by barbarians in A.D. 267, the Agora (which means "gathering place") was the hub of all commercial, political, and social life in Athens, as well as home to much of its religious activity. Everybody who was anybody in ancient Athens spent time here, from Socrates and Plato to a visiting missionary named Paul. Little survives from the classical Agora. Other than one very well-preserved temple and a rebuilt stoa, it's a field of humble ruins. But that makes it a quiet, un-crowded spot to wander and get a feel for the ancients.

ORIENTATION

Cost: €4 or covered by €12 Acropolis ticket (which you can buy here; see page 123).

Hours: Daily May-Aug 8:00-20:00, Sept until 18:45, Oct until 18:00, Nov-April until 15:00, last entry 30 minutes before closing. The Agora Museum inside has the same hours, except on Mon when it opens at 11:00.

Getting There: From Monastiraki (Metro line 1/green or line 3/blue), walk a block south (uphill, toward the Acropolis). Turn right on Adrianou street, and follow the pedestrian-only, café-lined street along the railroad tracks for about 200 yards. The Agora entrance is on your left, across from a small yellow church. The entrance can be hard to spot: It's where a path crosses over the railroad tracks (look for a small, pale-yellow sign that says *Ministry of Culture—Ancient Agora*).

Compass Points: The Agora entrance is north; the Acropolis is south.

Information: Panels with printed descriptions of the ruins are scattered helpfully throughout the site; tel. 210-321-0180, www.culture.gr.

Audio Tour: You can download a free audio version of this tour for your mobile device via www.ricksteves.com/audioeurope, iTunes, or the Rick Steves Audio Europe smartphone app.

Cuisine Art: Picnicking is not allowed in the Agora. Plenty of cafés and tavernas line busy Adrianou street near the Agora entrance, and more good eateries front the Apostolou Pavlou pedestrian walkway that hems in the western edge of the Agora, in the Thissio district (see the Eating chapter).

Starring: A well-preserved temple, a rebuilt stoa, three monumental statues, and the ruins of the civilization that built the Western world.

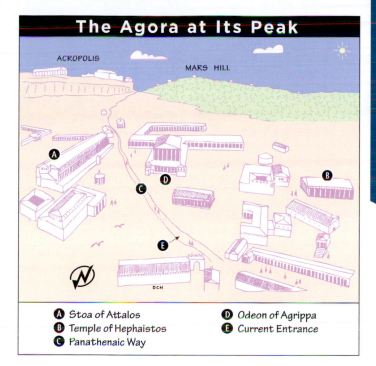

The Agora at Its Peak

A Stoa of Attalos
B Temple of Hephaistos
C Panathenaic Way
D Odeon of Agrippa
E Current Entrance

THE TOUR BEGINS

Entering the site from the Adrianou street entrance, belly up to the illustration at the top of the ramp that shows Athens at its peak. Face the Acropolis (to the south), look out over the expanse of ruins and trees, and get oriented.

The long column-lined building to the left is the reconstructed Stoa of Attalos (#13 on the illustration). To your right, atop a hill (the view is likely blocked by trees) is the well-preserved Temple of Hephaistos (#20). The pathway called the Panathenaic Way (#21) runs from the Agora's entrance up to the Acropolis. Directly ahead of you are three tall statue-columns—part of what was once the Odeon of Agrippa (#12).

Panathenaic Way cutting through the Agora.

Statue-columns and the distant Acropolis.

In the distance, the Agora's far end is bordered by hills. From left to right are the Acropolis (#1), the Areopagus ("Hill of Ares," or Mars Hill, #2), and Pnyx Hill (#3).

Although the illustration implies that you're standing somewhere behind the Stoa Poikile ("Painted Stoa," #28), in fact you are located closer to the heart of the Agora, near the Altar of the Twelve Gods (#26). In ancient times, that altar was considered the geographical center of Athens, from which distances were measured. Today, the area north of the altar (and north of today's illustration) remains largely unexcavated and inaccessible to tourists, taken over by the railroad tracks and Adrianou street. The computer terminal (just to your right) is an impractical boondoggle that has never really worked—the result of corrupt cronyism that is so frustrating to Athenians. Someone made a fortune setting these things up.

This self-guided tour starts at the Stoa of Attalos (with its museum), then crosses the Agora to the Temple of Hephaistos, returning to the Panathenaic Way via three giant statues. Finally, we'll head up the Panathenaic Way toward the Acropolis.

▶ *Walk to the bottom of the ramp at your left for a better view. Find a shady spot to ponder...*

❶ The Agora at Its Peak, circa A.D. 150

What lies before you now is a maze of ruins—the remains of many centuries of buildings.

A millennium before the time of Socrates, during the Mycenaean Period (around 1400 B.C.), this area held the oldest cemetery in Athens. Later, the Agora was developed into an open marketplace—a rectangular area (about 100 yards by 200 yards), bordered by hills. Over time, that

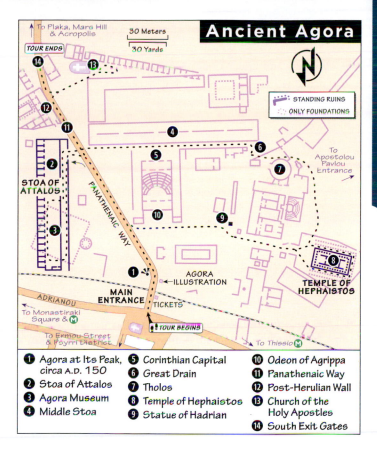

Ancient Agora

To Plaka, Mars Hill & Acropolis

TOUR ENDS

30 Meters
30 Yards

STANDING RUINS
ONLY FOUNDATIONS

To Apostolou Pavlou Entrance

STOA OF ATTALOS

PANATHENAIC WAY

AGORA
←ILLUSTRATION

MAIN ENTRANCE

ADRIANOU

To Monastiraki Square & Ⓜ

To Ermou Street & Psyrri District

TICKETS

TOUR BEGINS

To Thissio Ⓜ

TEMPLE OF HEPHAISTOS

1. Agora at Its Peak, circa A.D. 150
2. Stoa of Attalos
3. Agora Museum
4. Middle Stoa
5. Corinthian Capital
6. Great Drain
7. Tholos
8. Temple of Hephaistos
9. Statue of Hadrian
10. Odeon of Agrippa
11. Panathenaic Way
12. Post-Herulian Wall
13. Church of the Holy Apostles
14. South Exit Gates

central square became surrounded by buildings, then filled in by more buildings. There were stoas like the (reconstructed) Stoa of Attalos (above on the left), used for shops and offices; temples such as the Temple of Hephaistos; and government buildings. Imagine the square framed by these buildings—made of gleaming white marble, fronted with columns, topped with red-tile roofs. The square itself was studded with trees and dotted with statues, fountains, and altars. Merchants sold goods from wooden market stalls.

The square buzzed with people—mostly men and lower-class working women, as the place was considered a bit vulgar for genteel matrons. Both men and women would be dressed in simple tunics (men's were knee-length, women's to the ankle). The Agora was the place to shop—to buy groceries, clothes, dishes, or to get your wagon wheel fixed. If you needed a zoning permit for your business, you came to the courthouse. You could make an offering to the gods at a number of temples and altars. At night, people attended plays and concerts, and the tavernas hummed with excited drinkers. Many people passed through here on their way to somewhere else, as this was the main intersection in town (and ancient Athens probably had a population of at least 100,000). The Agora was the center for speeches, political announcements, and demonstrations. On holidays, the parade ran down main street, the Panathenaic Way. At any time, this was the place to come to run into your friends, to engage in high-minded discussion with philosophers such as Socrates or Diogenes, or just to chat and hang out.

▶ *Head to the long, intact, colonnaded building on your left (entrance at the south/far end).*

❷ Stoa of Attalos

This stoa—an ancient shopping mall—was originally built by the Greek-loving King Attalos II of Pergamon (in modern-day Turkey, 159-138 B.C.) as a thank-you gift for the education he'd received in Athens. The building we see today is a faithful reconstruction built in the 1950s by the American School of Classical Studies.

This is a typical two-story stoa. Like many of the Agora's buildings, it's made of white Pentelic marble. The portico is 381 feet by 64 feet, supported on the ground floor by 45 Doric columns (outer layer) and 22 Ionic columns (inner layer). The upper story uses Ionic columns. This mix of Doric and Ionic was typical of buildings from the period.

Stoas, with their covered walkways, provided protection from sun and rain for shoppers and businesspeople. This one likely served as a commercial mall. The ground floor was divided by walls into 21 rooms that served as shops (it's now the museum). Upstairs were offices (which today house the American School of Classical Studies).

Like malls of today, the Agora's stoas were also social magnets.

Stoa of Attalos—reconstructed "mall."

The stoa now houses the Agora Museum.

Imagine ancient Greeks (their hard labor being done by slaves) lounging here, enjoying the shade of the portico. The pillars were designed to encourage people to lean against them (just as you may be doing right now)—with fluting starting only above six feet—for the comfort of philosophers.

▶ *The Stoa of Attalos houses the…*

❸ Agora Museum

This excellent little museum displays some choice rubble that helps bring the Agora to life. Before entering, enjoy the arcade. Near the fifth column, find the impressive sculpted head of a bearded man with a full head of hair. This **Head of a Triton** (c. A.D. 150) comes from one of the statues that decorated the Odeon of Agrippa. Three of his fellow statues are still standing (we'll see them soon).

Walk halfway down the arcade and step inside the museum (included with your Agora ticket). The museum's modest but engaging collection fills a single long hall. Look in the corner for the 1952 photo showing this spot before the reconstruction. This well-described chronological stroll through art from 3200 B.C. gives you a glimpse of life in ancient Athens. Along the hall on the left, big panels show the Agora and Acropolis during each age, allowing you to follow their physical evolution.

The first few cases show off **jars** from various eras, including Neolithic (from the era when the Agora was first inhabited) and Geometric (with hash-mark designs). Much of this exhibit shows how pottery evolved over time. Usually painted red and black, pottery was a popular export product for the sea-trading Greeks. The earliest featured geometric patterns (eighth century B.C.), then a painted black silhouette on the natural orange clay, then a red figure on a black background.

An ancient commode.

Clay ballot voting Aristides out of Athens.

Cases 30-32 (on right), with items from **early democracy,** are especially interesting. The "voting machine" (*kleroterion,* case 31) was used to choose council members. Citizens put their name in the slots, then black and white balls went into the tube to randomly select who would serve (much like your turn in jury duty). Below the machine are bronze ballots from the fourth century. The pottery shards with names painted on them (*ostrakan,* case 30) were used as ballots in voting to ostracize someone accused of corruption or tyranny. Find the ones marked ΘΕΜΙSΘΟΚLΕS ΝΕΟΚLΕΟS (item #37) and ΑRΙSSΤΕΙΔΕS (item #17). During the Golden Age, Themistocles and Aristides were rivals (in both politics and romance) who served Athens honorably but were also exiled in political power struggles.

In case 32, see the *klepsydra* ("water thief")—a **water clock** used to time speeches at Council meetings. It took six minutes for the 1.7 gallons to drain out. A gifted orator truly was good to the last drop...but not a second longer.

Across the hall (under the banner, between cases 68 and 67) is the so-called **Stele of Democracy** (c. 336 B.C.). This stone monument is inscribed with a decree outlawing tyranny. Above, a relief carving shows Lady Democracy crowning a man representing the Athenian people.

Next to that (in case 67) is a **bronze shield** captured from defeated Spartans in the tide-turning Battle of Sphacteria, which gave Athens the upper hand in the first phase of the Peloponnesian War.

In the middle of the room, find the case of **coins.** These drachmas and tetradrachmas feature Athena with her helmet. In Golden Age times, a drachma was roughly a day's wage. The ancients put coins like these in the mouth of a deceased person as payment for the underworld ferryman

Charon to carry the soul safely across the River Styx. Coin #7, with the owl, was a four-drachma piece; that same owl is on Greece's €1 coin today.

▶ *Exiting the museum at the far end of the arcade (where there's a WC and a water fountain), backtrack to the southern end of the stoa (where you entered), then cross the main road and continue straight (west) along the lane, across the middle of the Agora. You're walking alongside the vast ruins (on your left) of what once was the...*

❹ Middle Stoa

Stretching clear across the Agora, this was part of a large complex of buildings that likely served as a big mall of shops and offices. It was a long, narrow rectangle (about 500 feet by 60 feet), similar to the reconstructed Stoa of Attalos you just left. You can still see the two lines of stubby column fragments that once supported the roof, a few stone steps, and (at the far end) some of the reddish foundation blocks. Constructed around 180 B.C., this stoa occupied what had been open space in the center of the Agora.

▶ *Midway down the lane (just before the wooden ramp), you'll come across a huge and frilly upper cap, or capital, of a column.*

❺ Corinthian Capital: The Center of the Agora

This capital (dating from the fourth century B.C.) once stood here atop a colossal column, one of a dozen columns that lined the monumental entrance to the Odeon of Agrippa, a theater that extended northward from the Middle Stoa. (We'll learn more about the Odeon later.) The capital's elaborate acanthus-leaf decoration is an early example of the Corinthian order. The style was rarely used in Greek buildings but became wildly popular with the Romans.

From here, look back toward the entrance, overlooking what was once the vacant expanse at the center of the Agora. In 400 B.C., there was no Middle Stoa and no Odeon—this was all open space. As Athens grew, the space was increasingly filled in with shops and monuments.

▶ *Continue westward (over a wooden bridge) across the Agora. Near the end of the Middle Stoa, you'll pass a gray well—still in its original spot and worn by the grooves of ropes. From here, look up at the Acropolis, where the towering but empty pedestal once sported the Monument of Agrippa, a grand statue with four horses. Mars Hill, likely lined with tourists, is where the Apostle Paul famously preached the Gospel (described*

This leaf-ornamented Corinthian capital once topped a column at the Roman-built Odeon.

on page 122). Below the Erechtheion are broken columns shoring up the side of the hill. These were rubble from the Mycenaean temples that were destroyed by the Persians. Past the well, jog to the right and cross the ditch over the wooden bridge. This ditch is part of the waterworks system known as the...

⑥ Great Drain

Dug in the fifth century B.C. and still functioning today, these ditches channel rainwater runoff from the southern hills through the Agora. Here at the southwest corner of the Agora, two main collection ditches meet and join. You can see exposed parts of the stone-lined ditch. The well we just passed was also part of this system.

▶ *Just over the wooden bridge is a 60-foot-across round footprint with a stubby column in its center. This is the...*

❼ Tholos

This rotunda-shaped building housed Athens' rulers. Built around 465 B.C., it was originally ringed with six Ionic columns that held up a conical roof. In the middle was an altar (marked today by the broken column).

The fundamental unit of Athenian democracy was the Assembly, made up of the thousands of adult male citizens who could vote. Athenian citizens were organized into 10 tribes; in order to prevent the people living in any one geographical area from becoming dominant, each tribe was composed of citizens from the city, the coast, and inland areas. Each man in the Assembly was considered to be from one of these tribes. Though some Assembly meetings were held in the Agora's central square, the main assemblies were just uphill, on the slope of Pnyx Hill.

The City Council also met in the Agora. The Council consisted of 500 men (50 from each of the 10 tribes) who were chosen from the Assembly by lottery to serve a one-year term. The Council proposed and debated legislation, but since Athens practiced direct (not representational) democracy, all laws eventually had to be approved by the whole Assembly. The Council chose 50 ministers who ran the day-to-day affairs.

The *tholos* was the headquarters, offices, and meeting hall for the 50 ministers. Many also lived and ate here, since the law required that at least a third of these ministers be on the premises at all times. The *tholos* housed the official weights and measures. Any shopper in the Agora could use these to check whether a butcher or tailor was shortchanging them. As the center of government, the *tholos* was also a kind of temple to the city. The altar in the middle held an eternal flame, representing the hearth of the extended "family" that was Athens.

▶ *Beyond and above the tholos is the hill-capping Temple of Hephaistos. To reach it, climb the stairs to the left and go through the trees, pausing along the way at a viewpoint with a chart.*

❽ Temple of Hephaistos (a.k.a. the Theseion or Theseum)

One of the best-preserved and most typical of all temples, this is textbook Golden Age architecture. Started in 450 B.C., it was built at Athens' peak as part of the massive reconstruction of the Agora after invading Persians destroyed the city (480 B.C.). But the temple wasn't completed and dedicated until 415 B.C., as work stalled when the Greeks started erecting the great buildings of the Acropolis. Notice how the frieze around the outside of the building was only finished on the side facing the Agora (it's blank elsewhere).

As a classic "peripteral" or "peristyle" temple (like the Parthenon), the building is surrounded by columns—6 on each end, 13 on the long sides (counting the corners twice). Also like the Parthenon, it's made of Pentelic marble in the Doric style, part of Pericles' vision of harking back to Athens' austere, solid roots. But the Temple of Hephaistos is only about half the size of the grand Parthenon and with fewer refinements (compared to the Parthenon's elaborate carvings and fancy math).

The temple's entrance was on the east end (the one facing the Agora). Priests would enter through the six columns here, into a covered portico (note the coffered ceiling). Next came a three-sided alcove called the *pronaos,* or "pre-temple." From there, you'd continue into the central hall *(cella),* which once housed large bronze statues of Hephaistos, the blacksmith god, and Athena, patroness of Athens and of pottery. In ancient times, the temple was surrounded by metalworking and pottery shops, before the Romans replaced them with gardens, similar to today's. Behind the *cella* (the west end) is another three-sided alcove, matching the *pronaos.*

The carved reliefs (frieze and metopes) that run around the upper part of the building are only partly done. Some panels may have been left unfinished, others may have once been decorated with painted (not sculpted) scenes, and a few panels have been removed and put in the Agora Museum.

At the end overlooking the Agora, look between the six columns and up at the frieze above the *pronaos* to find scenes of Theseus battling his enemies, trying to unite Athens. Theseus would go on to free Athens from

The well-preserved Temple of Hephaistos.

Frieze of centaurs battling humans.

the dominance of Crete by slaying the bull-headed Minotaur. To this day, Athenians call the temple the "Theseion" because the frieze decorations led them to mistakenly believe that it once held the remains of the mythical hero Theseus.

Walk around behind the temple, to the far (west) end. The frieze above the three-sided alcove depicts the mythological battle between the Lapith tribe and centaurs during a wedding feast. Other scenes you'll see around the building (there are many interpretations) include Hercules (his labors and deification) and the birth of Erichthonios (one of Athens' first kings, who was born when spurned Hephaistos tried to rape Athena, spilled semen, and instead impregnated Gaia, the earth).

In A.D. 1300, the temple was converted into the Church of Agios Georgios, dedicated to Greece's patron saint, George, and given the vaulted ceiling that survives today. During the Ottoman occupation, the Turks kept the church open but permitted services to be held only once each year (on St. George's Day). Because it was continually in use, the temple-turned-church is remarkably well-preserved.

▶ *Note that there's a "back door" exit nearby for those wanting to take the smooth, paved walkway up to the Acropolis, rather than the rough climb above the Agora. (To find the exit, face the back of the temple, turn right, and follow the path to the green gate, which deposits you on the inviting, café-lined Apostolou Pavlou pedestrian drag. From here, you can turn left and walk up toward the Acropolis.)*

But there's still more to see in the Agora. Wind your way down the hill (east) and find the headless...

🟠 Statue of Hadrian (Second Century A.D.)

The first Roman emperor to wear a beard (previously a Greek fashion), Hadrian (r. A.D. 117-138) was a Grecophile and benefactor of Athens. Notice the insignia on the breastplate. There's Romulus and Remus, being suckled by the she-wolf who supports Athena on her back. This was Hadrian's vision—that by conquering Greece, Rome actually saved it. Hadrian was nicknamed Graecula ("The Little Greek") for his love of Greek philosophy, literature, and a handsome Greek teenager named Antinous. Hadrian personally visited Athens, where he financed new construction, including Hadrian's Arch, the Library of Hadrian, the Temple of Olympian Zeus (which had been started by the Greeks), and a planned neighborhood called Hadrianopolis. (For more on these sights, see the ⭐ Athens

Roman emperor Hadrian loved Greek culture.   Triton fronting the Odeon of Agrippa.

City Walk chapter.) Hadrian's legacy endures. The main street through the Plaka is now called Adrianou—"Hadrian's" street.

▶ *Farther along, the lane passes three giants on four pedestals, which once guarded the...*

⑩ Odeon of Agrippa (a.k.a. the "Palace of the Giants")

This theater/concert hall, once fronted by a line of six fierce Triton statues (of which just three survived), was the centerpiece of the Agora during the Roman era.

A plaque explains the history of this building: During the Golden Age, this site was simply open space in the very center of the Agora. The *odeon* (a venue designed mainly for musical performances) was built by the Roman general and governor Marcus Agrippa in the time of Caesar Augustus (around 15 B.C.), when Greece was a Roman-controlled province. For the theater-loving Greeks and their Greek-culture-loving masters, the *odeon* was a popular place. Two stories tall and built into the natural slope of the hill, it could seat more than a thousand people.

Back then, the entrance was on the south side (near the Middle Stoa), and these Triton statues didn't exist yet. Patrons entered from the south, walking through two rows of monumental columns, topped by Corinthian capitals. After the lobby, they emerged at the top row of a 20-tier, bowl-shaped auditorium, looking down on an orchestra and stage paved with multicolored marble and decorated with statues. The sightlines were great because the roof, spanning 82 feet, had no internal support columns. One can only assume that, in its heyday, the *odeon* hosted plays by Aristophanes, Euripides, and Sophocles, plus lute concerts, poetry readings, and more lowbrow Roman-oriented entertainment.

Around A.D. 150, the famously unsupported roof collapsed. By then, Athens had a bigger, better performance venue (the Odeon of Herodes Atticus, on the other side of the Acropolis—see page 48), so the Odeon of Agrippa was rebuilt at half the size as a 500-seat lecture hall. The new entrance was here on the north side, fronted by six colossal statues serving as pillars. Only two tritons (with fish tails), a giant (snake's tail), and an empty pedestal remain.

The building was burned to the ground in the Herulian invasion of A.D. 267 (explained later, under "Post-Herulian Wall"). Around A.D. 400, a large palace was built here, which also served as the university (or "gymnasium," which comes from the Greek word for "naked"—young men exercised in the buff during PE here). It lasted until the Constantinople-based Emperor Justinian closed all the pagan schools in A.D. 529. A plaque under the first statue gives more information.

▶ *Continue to the main road, where you'll see we've made a loop. Now turn right and start up toward the Acropolis on the...*

⑪ Panathenaic Way

The Panathenaic Way was Athens' main street. It started at the main city gate (the Dipylon Gate, near the Keramikos Cemetery), cut diagonally through the Agora's main square, and wound up to the Acropolis—two-thirds of a mile in all. The Panathenaic Way was the primary north-south road, and here in the Agora it intersected with the main east-west road to the port of Piraeus. Though some stretches were paved, most of it (then as now) was just packed gravel. It was lined with important temples, businesses, and legal buildings.

During the Panathenaic Festival (July-Aug), this was the main parade route. Every year on Athena's birthday, Greeks celebrated by giving her statue a new dress, called a *peplos.* A wheeled float carrying the *peplos* was pushed up this street. Thousands participated—some dancing, some on horseback, others just walking—while spectators watched from wooden grandstands erected along the way. When the parade reached the Acropolis, the new dress was ceremonially presented to Athena and used to adorn her life-size statue at the Erechtheion. Every fourth year was a special celebration, when Athenians created an enormous *peplos* for the 40-foot statue in the Parthenon. Today's tourists use the same path to connect the Agora and the Acropolis.

Walk the Panathenaic Way, the same street strolled by Socrates, Plato, and today's tourists.

▶ *Continue up the Panathenaic Way, past the Stoa of Attalos. Along the left-hand side are several crude walls and column fragments.*

⑫ Post-Herulian Wall

This wall marks the beginning of the end of classical Athens.

In A.D. 267, the barbarian Herulians sailed down from the Black Sea and utterly devastated Athens. (The crumbling Roman Empire was helpless to protect its provinces.) The Herulians burned most of the Agora's buildings to the ground, leaving it in ashes.

As soon as the Herulians left, the surviving Athenians began hastily throwing up this wall—cobbled together from rubble—to keep future invaders at bay. They used anything they could find: rocks, broken columns, statues, frieze fragments, all thrown together without mortar to make a wall 30 feet high and 10 feet thick. Archaeologists recognize pieces scavenged from destroyed buildings, such as the Stoa of Attalos and the Odeon of Agrippa.

Up until this point, the Agora had always been rebuilt after invasions (such as the Persians in 480 B.C. and Romans in 89 B.C.); but after the Herulian invasion, the Agora never recovered as a public space. What remained suffered through a Slavic invasion in A.D. 580. By A.D. 700, it was a virtual ghost town.

▶ *Next came the Christians. On the right is the...*

⑬ Church of the Holy Apostles

This charming little church with the lantern-like dome marks the Agora's revival. Built around A.D. 1000, it commemorates St. Paul's teaching in the Agora (see page 122). Under protection from the Christian rulers of

Post-Herulian wall to keep barbarians out.

Holy Apostles church adds a Christian layer.

Byzantium (in Constantinople, modern-day Istanbul), Athens—and the Agora—slowly recovered from centuries of invasions and neglect. The church was built on the ruins of an ancient nymphaeum, or temple atop a sacred spring, and became one of many Christian churches that served the booming populace of Byzantine Athens.

This church was the prototype for later Athenian churches: a Greek-cross floor plan with four equal arms, topped by a dome and featuring windows with tall horseshoe-shaped arches. (The narthex, or entrance, was added later, spoiling the four equal arms.) Enter around the far side. It contains some interesting 18th-century Byzantine-style frescoes. From the center, look up at Jesus as *Pantocrator* at the top of the dome, and see the icon on the altar and the faded frescoes on the walls. The uniform chipping on the surface of the frescoes was part of a process designed to rough it up so a new coat of whitewashing could adhere. Notice the remains of the marble altar screen with wide-open spaces—frames that once held icons.

▶ *Our tour is over. There are three exits: the gate you used to enter, at Adrianou street; the "back door" gate behind the Temple of Hephaistos; and* 🄴 *the* **south gate** *next to the Church of the Holy Apostles. To go to the Acropolis, exit through the gate by the church and head straight up the hill.*

Acropolis Museum Tour

Μουσείο Ακρόπολης

Athens' Acropolis Museum, opened in 2009, was custom-built to show-case artifacts from the Acropolis—the Parthenon sculptures, the original caryatids from the Erechtheion, and much more—complemented by modern exhibits about the Acropolis. The state-of-the-art building that houses the collection is the boldest symbol yet of today's Athens.

The museum also serves as a sort of 21st-century Trojan horse, intended to lure the famous Parthenon sculptures (the Elgin Marbles) away from London's British Museum and back to Athens. So far, Britain has refused to give in, for fear of setting a precedent...and getting "me, too" notices from Italy, Egypt, Iran, Iraq, and other nations wanting to reclaim the missing pieces of their cultural heritage.

ORIENTATION

Cost: €5.

Hours: Tue-Sun 8:00-20:00, Fri until 22:00, closed Mon, last entry 30 minutes before closing.

Getting There: It's the giant modern building facing the south side of the Acropolis from across the broad Dionysiou Areopagitou pedestrian drag. The museum is next to the Akropoli Metro stop (line 2/red).

Information: Museum archaeologists (with red badges) can answer questions, and a 13-minute video plays continuously in the atrium on Level 3; tel. 210-900-0900, www.theacropolismuseum.gr.

Length of This Tour: Allow 1.5 hours.

Photography: Not allowed inside.

Services: A café and gift shop are on the ground floor (Level 0); Level 2 has a pricey but good restaurant, a bookstore, and great views.

Starring: Marble masterpieces from one of the most influential works of art in human history.

THE TOUR BEGINS

The striking, glassy building—designed by Swiss-born, New York-based architect Bernard Tschumi—gives a postmodern jolt to Athens' otherwise staid, mid-century-concrete cityscape, even as it echoes the ancient history all around it. Its two lower levels are aligned with the foundations of ancient ruins discovered beneath the building (which are exposed and still being excavated). The top floor sits askew, imitating the orientation of the Parthenon. A long terrace extends over the main entry, with café tables stretching toward panoramic views of the Acropolis. The glass walls of the museum not only maximize the amount of natural light inside, but are also designed to "disappear," focusing attention away from the building and onto the statuary and views of the Acropolis itself.

Visitors enter into a grand lobby. The ground floor (Level 0) has the ticket office, WCs, museum shop, and temporary exhibits. To proceed chronologically through the exhibits, you'd start with the Archaic collection on Level 1, then go upstairs (to the top floor—Level 3) for the Parthenon section, then back down to Level 1 for Hellenistic and Roman sculpture. But for this tour, we'll do the small Hellenistic and Roman section as an out-of-chronological-sequence side-trip from the Archaic and Classical sections, and let the top-floor Parthenon sculptures be our finale.

▶ *After going through the turnstiles, head up the long, glass...*

Ramp

Pause to look through the glass floor at the ancient ruins being excavated beneath the museum. While the major buildings of ancient Athens were at the Acropolis and Agora, this was a neighborhood of everyday houses and shops. Appropriately, the ramp is lined with artifacts that were found in the sanctuaries on the slopes leading up to the Parthenon. Many of these fifth-century B.C. artifacts owe their well-preserved state to having been buried with their owners.

Among the ramp's highlights is case #5, which takes you step by step through marriage rituals in ancient Athens. Freestanding cases mid-ramp give insight into the similarities between ancient Greek pagan worship rituals and later Christian styles. One has Christian-looking votives thanking the gods for prayers answered. On the right, just below the stairs, is an offering box (like you see in churches today); this one stood at the Sanctuary

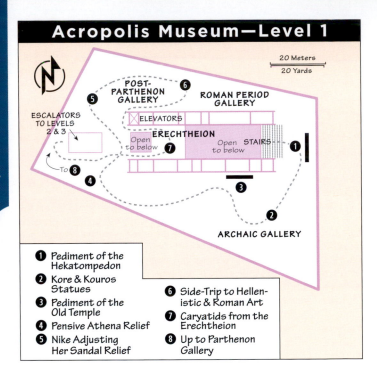

Acropolis Museum—Level 1

20 Meters
20 Yards

POST-PARTHENON GALLERY

ROMAN PERIOD GALLERY

ESCALATORS TO LEVELS 2 & 3

ELEVATORS

ERECHTHEION

Open to below

Open to below   STAIRS

To

ARCHAIC GALLERY

❶ Pediment of the Hekatompedon
❷ Kore & Kouros Statues
❸ Pediment of the Old Temple
❹ Pensive Athena Relief
❺ Nike Adjusting Her Sandal Relief
❻ Side-Trip to Hellenistic & Roman Art
❼ Caryatids from the Erechtheion
❽ Up to Parthenon Gallery

of Aphrodite. To assure a good marriage, you'd have been wise to pop in a silver drachma.

Level 1

▸ *Climb the stairs at the top of the ramp toward a collection of statues.*

Pediment of the Hekatompedon (570 B.C.)

Three temples of Athena have occupied the spot where the Parthenon stands today. These statues once adorned the Hekatompedon, the first of those temples. On the left, Hercules fights a sea monster (Triton). In the center are the scant remains of two lions killing a bull. To the right, look-

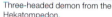

Three-headed demon from the Hekatompedon.

Female kore statue with archaic smile.

ing like the Three Musketeers, is a three-headed demon with a snake tail holding the three elements (air, water, fire).

▶ *Turn right and enter a gallery flooded with daylight.*

Kore and Kouros Statues

In this column-lined gallery stand several kore (female) and kouros (male) statues. They sport the characteristic stiff poses, braided hair, generic faces, and mysterious smiles of the Archaic era (c. 650-480 B.C.). For more on Archaic statues, see page 105.

The men are generally naked, showing off buff and toned bodies. The bearded dudes are adults, while boys are beardless. Women are modestly clothed—except for Aphrodite. If you can find one naked breast in this gallery, it belongs to the goddess of love. The women pull up their robes as if readying to take a step. Before the coming of Golden Age realism, this was a crude way to suggest motion. These figures are almost always holding something. That's because the Greeks believed you shouldn't approach the gods without a gift of some kind. The equestrian statues represent the upper class, those wealthy elites who owned horses.

▶ *Halfway down the gallery, on the right against the interior wall, is the...*

Pediment of the Old Temple (Archaios Naos)

This decorated the short-lived temple to Athena that succeeded the Hekatompedon. The still-under-construction building was leveled by invading Persians in 480 B.C., paving the way for the Parthenon to be built. In the center, a large statue of Athena, dressed in an ankle-length cloak, strides forward, brandishing a snake as she attacks a giant, who sprawls backward onto his bum. These figures were part of a scene depicting the "Gods versus Giants" battle atop the temple.

The glass case nearby displays fragments with burn marks, traces of the fire set by the Persians. The pesky Persians invaded Greece several times over a 50-year period (c. 499-449 B.C.). On the plus side, the wars forced Greeks to band together, and Athens emerged as a dominant naval power. Athenians rebuilt the Acropolis as a symbol of rebirth, with the Parthenon as its centerpiece.

▶ *Continue down the gallery. Near the end, look for a well-preserved marble relief placed in front of a concrete pillar.*

Pensive Athena Relief (460 B.C.)

The goddess, dressed in a helmet and belted *peplos,* rests her forehead thoughtfully on her spear. While called "pensive," some think she was actually meant to be mourning the deaths of her citizens in the Persian War.

Enjoying the statuary in this hall, you can trace the evolution of Greek art from the static Archaic period to the mastery of the body as a living thing, free and full of movement, that we see in the Golden Age. In the Classical style of fifth-century B.C. Greece, the spine moves with the hips realistically.

▶ *Turn right and walk past a bank of elevators. Continue past an open gallery with some statuesque women (we'll visit them in a minute). After the second bank of elevators, look for a series of four squarish marble slabs on your left.*

Nike Adjusting Her Sandal Relief (c. 410 B.C.)

This relief originally decorated the Temple of Athena Nike (which stands

Pensive Athena, dressed for battle.

Nike lifts her leg to adjust her sandal.

near the entrance to the Acropolis). Nike figures had a better chance of survival through the ages than other statues, because anti-pagan Christian vandals mistook the winged Nikes for angels. Nearby is a display containing more chunks of the Temple of Athena Nike. You'll see toes gripping rocks, windblown robes, and realistically twisted bodies—exuberant, life-filled carvings signaling Athens' emergence from the Persian War.

▶ *Turn right and go up the long gallery for a...*

Side-Trip to Hellenistic and Roman Art

Before heading upstairs, continue around on this floor to the small stretch of statues from the Hellenistic and Roman period. The head of Alexander the Great, on a square pillar in the center of the gallery, is a rare original, likely sculpted from life (336 B.C.). Alexander's upper lip curls, and his thick hair sprouts from the center of his forehead. When he died in 323 B.C., this Macedonian had conquered Greece, embraced its customs, and spread Greek culture throughout the Mediterranean world and as far east as India.

Nearby, a model shows the Acropolis as it looked in Roman times. The room also holds something that resembles a dirty soccer ball covered with graffiti. It's actually a spooky marble sphere etched with mysterious magic symbols (Roman, second or third century A.D.).

▶ *Now turn around, retracing your steps, and turn left at the bank of elevators. Around the corner, on their own, as if starring in their own revue on a beautifully lit stage, are the...*

Caryatids from the Erechtheion

Here stand four of the original six lady-columns that once supported the roof of the prestigious Erechtheion temple. (The six on the Acropolis today are copies; another original is in London's British Museum, and the last one is in France.) Despite their graceful appearance, these sculptures were fully functional structurally. Each has a fluted column for a leg, a capital-like hat, and buttressing locks of hair in the back. The caryatids were modeled on and named after the famously upright women of Karyai, near Sparta.

Time and the elements have ravaged these maidens. As recently as the 17th century (see the engravings), they had fragile arms holding baskets of flowers and jugs for ritual wine. Until the 1950s (before modern smog), their worn-down faces had crisp noses and mouths. In a half-century of Industrial Age pollution, they experienced more destruction than in the previous 2,000 years. But their future looks brighter now that they've been brought indoors out of the acidic air, cleaned up with a laser, and safely preserved for future generations. (For more on the caryatids in their original location, see page 60.)

There's a glass floor overhead; don't look up, out of respect for any female visitors wearing dresses above you.

▶ *Walk out of the Caryatid Gallery to the end of the building and ride the escalators up. Keep going up past Level Two, which has a restaurant and awesome view terrace. Head for the top floor—it's the reason you're here.*

The original Erechtheion caryatids—ravaged by time and pollution—retain their elegant dignity.

Level 3

▶ *Before entering the Parthenon Gallery, sit in the atrium and enjoy the video, which covers the temple's 2,500-year history, including a not-so-subtle jab at how Lord Elgin got the Marbles and made off with them to England. For more on Lord Elgin, see page 65.*

Parthenon Models

Two models show how the west and east pediment statues (which are mostly fragments today) would have looked in their prime.

The east pediment (the model on the right) features Nike crowning newly born Athena with a wreath of olive branches. Zeus' head is split open, allowing Athena, the goddess of wisdom, to rise from his brain fully grown and fully armed, inaugurating the Golden Age of Athens. The other gods at this Olympian banquet—naked men and clothed women—are astounded by the amazing event. At the far left, Helios' four horses are doing their morning chore, dragging the sun out of the sea. And on the far right, the sun follows the horses back as it sets into the sea again.

The west pediment model (on the left) shows Athena and Poseidon competing for Athens' favor by giving gifts to the city. Poseidon spurts water (beneath him) and Athena presents an olive tree (behind). A big, heavenly audience looks on. Had Poseidon bested Athena, you'd be in Poseidonia today instead of Athens. Among the bystanders—tucked into the left corner of the pediment—are the mythical king of Athens and his daughters (Kekrops and Pandrosos). Passed over by Lord Elgin, their now headless and limbless statues are on display in the next room.

▶ *Leave the atrium and enter the huge gallery.*

The Parthenon Frieze

In the center of the room stands the museum's highlight—a life-size mock-up of the 525-foot frieze that once wrapped all the way around the outside of the Parthenon. The relief panels depict the annual parade, the Panathenaic procession, in which citizens climbed up the Acropolis to celebrate the birth of the city. Circle the perimeter and watch the parade unfold.

Men on horseback, chariots, musicians, children, and animals for sacrifice are all part of the grand parade, all heading in the same direction—uphill. Prance on. At the heart of the procession are maidens dressed in pleated robes. They shuffle along, carrying gifts for the gods, including

Scene from the 525-foot Parthenon frieze, depicting the Panathenaic parade up the Acropolis.

incense burners, along with jugs of wine and bowls to pour out offerings. The procession culminates in the presentation of the *peplos* to Athena, as the gods look on.

Notice the details—for example, the muscles and veins in the horses' legs and the intricate folds in the cloaks and dresses. Some panels have holes drilled in them, where accessories such as gleaming bronze reins were fitted to heighten the festive look. Of course, all of these panels were originally painted in realistic colors. As you move along, notice that, despite the bustle of figures posed every which way, the frieze has one unifying element—all of the people's heads are at the same level, creating a single ribbon around the Parthenon.

Of the 525-foot-long frieze, the museum owns only 32 feet of original panels. These parts were already so acid-worn in 1801 that Lord Elgin didn't bother taking them. Filling in the gaps in this jigsaw puzzle are white plaster replicas of panels still in London's British Museum (marked BM), in Paris' Louvre, and in Copenhagen. Blank spaces represent the panels that were lost forever. Small 17th-century engravings show how the frieze looked before the 1687 explosion that devastated the Parthenon.

▶ *Now stroll through the gallery and look out the windows. Take a moment to...*

Ponder the Parthenon

There's the Parthenon itself, perched on the adjacent hilltop. The Parthenon is one of the most influential works humankind has ever created. For 2,500 years, it's inspired generations of architects, sculptors, painters, engineers, and visitors from around the globe. Here in the Acropolis Museum, you can experience the power of this cultural landmark. The people of Athens relish this museum. Local guides grow taller with every visit, knowing that Greece finally has a suitable place to preserve and share the best of its artistic heritage.

▶ *On your way down, stop by the restaurant on Level 2 for its exterior terrace and an amazing view of the Acropolis.*

The museum's view restaurant—aged wines and the ancient Parthenon.

National Archaeological Museum Tour

Εθνικό Αρχαιολογικό Μουσείο

The National Archaeological Museum is the top ancient Greek art collection anywhere in the world. Ancient Greece set the tone for all Western art that followed, and this museum lets you trace its evolution, with beautifully displayed and described exhibits from 7000 B.C. to A.D. 500. You'll see the rise and fall of Greece's civilizations: the Minoans, Mycenaeans, those of Archaic Greece, the Classical Age, and Alexander the Great, and then the Romans. Watch Greek sculpture evolve from prehistoric Barbie dolls, to stiff Egyptian-style, to the *David*-like balance of the Golden Age, to wet T-shirt, buckin'-bronco Hellenistic, and finally, to the influence of the Romans.

ORIENTATION

Cost: €7; free for those 18 and under, on the first Sun of the month, and every Sun Nov-March.

Hours: May-mid-Sept Tue-Sun 8:00-20:00, Mon 13:30-20:00; mid-Sept-Oct Tue-Sun 8:00-19:00, Mon 13:30-20:00; Nov-April Tue-Sun 8:00-15:00, Mon 13:30-20:00; last entry 20 minutes before closing; tel. 210-821-7717, www.namuseum.gr.

Getting There: The museum is a mile north of the Plaka at 28 Oktovriou (a.k.a. Patission) #44. A taxi between the Plaka and the museum is a steal at €4. The nearest Metro stop is Omonia (as you exit, follow signs to *28 Oktovriou/28 October Street,* and walk seven blocks to the museum). Or you can catch bus #035 from Athinas street, just north of Monastiraki, which drops you off around the corner from the museum, or bus #224 from Vasilissis Sofias (next to Syntagma Square), which stops kitty-corner from the museum.

Tours: While there are no audioguides, live guides hang out in the lobby waiting to give you a €50, hour-long tour. You can download a **free audio version** of my tour for your mobile device via www.ricksteves.com/audioeurope, iTunes, or the Rick Steves Audio Europe smartphone app.

Length of This Tour: Allow two hours for this tour; more if you want to dig deeper.

Baggage Check: Free and required, except for small purses.

Services: A museum shop, WCs, and an inviting café surround a shady and restful courtyard in the lower level (to access from the main entrance lobby, take the stairs down behind ticket desk); these are easiest to access at the beginning or end of your museum tour.

Photography: Photos are allowed, but no flash or goofy poses in front of statues. The Greek museum board considers this disrespectful of the ancient culture and is very serious about it.

Starring: The gold Mask of Agamemnon, stately kouros and kore statues, the perfectly posed *Artemision Bronze,* the horse and jockey of Artemision, and the whole range of Greek art.

THE TOUR BEGINS

The collection is delightfully chronological. To sweep through Greek history, simply visit the numbered rooms in order. From the entrance lobby (Rooms 1-2), start with the rooms directly in front of you (Rooms 3-6), containing prehistoric and Mycenaean artifacts. Then circle clockwise around the building's perimeter on the ground floor (Rooms 7-31) to see the evolution of classical Greek statuary. Keep track of your ticket—you'll need to show it again to enter some of the exhibits.

This self-guided tour zeroes in on a few choice pieces that give an overview of the collection. Note that my descriptions here are brief—for more detail, read the excellent posted English information in each room.

▶ *From the entrance lobby, go straight ahead into the large central hall (Room 4). This first area—Rooms 3-6—is dedicated to prehistory (7000-1050 B.C.), including the treasures of the Mycenaeans. Start in the small side room to the right, Room 6. In several of this room's cases—including the one directly to the right as you enter—you'll find stiff marble figures with large heads.*

❶ Cycladic Figurines

Goddess, corpse, fertility figure, good-luck amulet, spirit guide, beloved ancestor, or Neolithic porn? No one knows for sure the purpose of these female figurines, which are older than the Egyptian pyramids. These statuettes were found all over Greece, particularly in the Cycladic Islands. The earliest Greeks may have worshipped a Great Mother earth goddess long before Zeus and company (variously called Gaia, Ge, Rhea, and other names), but it's not clear what connection she had, if any, with these

Cycladic figures—prehistoric Barbies?

Mask of Agamemnon—a Mycenaean treasure.

National Archaeological Museum

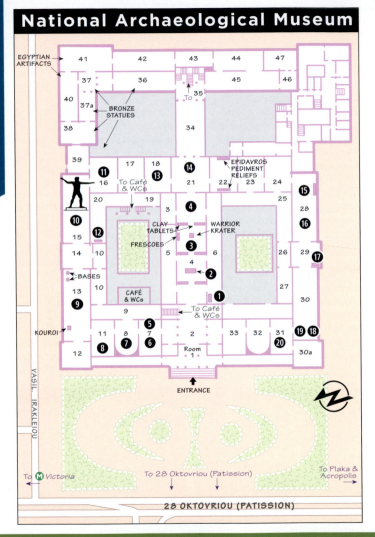

EGYPTIAN ARTIFACTS

BRONZE STATUES

To Café & WCs

EPIDAVROS PEDIMENT RELIEFS

CLAY TABLETS

FRESCOES

WARRIOR KRATER

CAFÉ & WCs

To Café & WCs

BASES

KOUROI

CAFÉ & WCs

Room 1

ENTRANCE

VASIL. IRAKLEIOU

To Ⓜ Victoria

To 28 Oktovriou (Patission)

To Plaka & Acropolis

28 OKTOVRIOU (PATISSION)

① Cycladic Figurines
② Mask of Agamemnon, Etc.
③ More Mycenaean Artifacts
④ Vapheio Cups
⑤ Dipylon Vase
⑥ Female Statue
⑦ Kouros from Sounion
⑧ Statue of a Kore
⑨ More Kouroi & Bases
⑩ Artemision Bronze
⑪ Attic Funerary Monuments
⑫ Athena Varvakeion Replica
⑬ Funeral Steles
⑭ Horse & Jockey of Artemision
⑮ Grave Relief of a Horse
⑯ Bronze Statue of a Youth
⑰ Philosopher Portrait Head
⑱ Fighting Gaul
⑲ Aphrodite, Pan & Eros
⑳ Emperor Augustus

statuettes. The ladies are always naked, usually with folded arms. The figures evolved over the years from flat-chested (c. 5000 B.C.), to violin-shaped, to skinny supermodels (c. 3000 B.C.). There is evidence that the eyes, lips, and ears were originally painted on.

▶ *Return to the long central hall (Room 4), divided into four sections. Here you'll find...*

② Mycenaean Treasures, Including the Mask of Agamemnon (#624), c. 1550 B.C.

Room 4 displays artifacts found in the ruins of the ancient fortress-city of Mycenae, 80 miles west of Athens. You'll see finely decorated swords, daggers, body armor, and jewelry, all found buried alongside bodies in Mycenaean graves. The objects' intricately hammered detail and the elaborate funeral arrangements point to the sophistication of this early culture.

In a glass case in the middle of the second section is the so-called Mask of Agamemnon. Made of gold and showing a man's bearded face, this mask was tied over the face of a dead man—note the tiny ear-holes for the string.

The Mycenaeans dominated southern Greece a thousand years before the Golden Age (1600-1200 B.C.). Their (real) history was lost in the misty era of Homer's (fanciful) legends of the Trojan War. Then Mycenae was unearthed in the 19th century by the German archaeologist Heinrich Schliemann (the Indiana Johannes of his era). Schliemann had recently discovered the real-life ruins of Troy (in western Turkey), and he was convinced that Mycenae was the city of the Greeks who'd conquered Troy. That much, at least, may be historically true. Schliemann went on to declare this funeral mask to be that of the legendary King Agamemnon, which *isn't* true, since the mask (c. 1550 B.C.) predates the fall of Troy (c. 1200 B.C.).

▶ *In the next section of Room 4, you'll find...*

❸ More Mycenaean Artifacts

A model of the Acropolis of Mycenae (left side) shows the dramatic hilltop citadel where many of these objects were unearthed. Clay tablets show the Mycenaean written language known as "Linear B," whose syllabic script (in which marks stand for syllables, as in Japanese) was cracked only 50 years ago.

At the back side of the display case in the center of this section is a painted, two-handled vase known as the Warrior Krater (#1426)— Schliemann's favorite find. A woman (far left) waves good-bye to a line of warriors heading off to war, with their fancy armor and duffle bags hanging from their spears. While this provided the world with its first glimpse of a Mycenaean soldier, it's a timeless scene with countless echoes across the generations.

▶ *In the center of the last section of Room 4 is a glass case displaying the...*

❹ Vapheio Cups (#1758 and #1759), c. 1600-1550 B.C.

The intricate metal-worked detail on #1758 shows a charging bull sending a guy head over heels. On #1759, you'll see a bull and a cow making eyes at each other, while the hind leg of another bull gets tied up by one good-looking cowboy. These realistic, joyous scenes are the product of

Warrior Krater shows soldiers off to war.

Vapheio cup—beautiful bovine love.

the two civilizations that made 15th-century B.C. Greece the wonder of Europe—the Mycenaeans and the Minoan culture of Crete.

But around 1450 B.C., the Minoan society collapsed, and Minoan artisans had to find work painting frescoes and making cups for the rising Mycenaean culture. Then around 1200 B.C., the Mycenaeans mysteriously disappeared from history's radar screen, plunging Greece into 400 years of Dark Ages (c. 1200-800 B.C.). Little survives from that chaotic time, so let's pick up the thread of history as Greece began to recover a few centuries later.

▶ *Backtrack to the entrance lobby and begin circling right (clockwise) around the perimeter of the building, starting in Room 7. After showing your ticket again to enter this room, look for the tall vase on your right.*

❺ Dipylon Vase (Monumental Attic Grave Amphora, #804), c. 750 B.C.

This ochre-and-black vase (see photo, next page), nearly four feet tall, is painted with a funeral scene. In the center, a dead man lies on a funeral bier, flanked by a line of mourners, who pull their hair in grief. It's far from realistic. The triangular torsos, square arms, circular heads, and bands of geometric patterns epitomize what's known as the Geometric Period (760-750 B.C.). A few realistic notes pop through, such as the raw emotions of the mourners and some grazing antelope (near the top).

After four centuries of Dark Ages and war, the Greeks of the eighth century B.C. were finally settling down, establishing cities, and expanding abroad (as seen on the map behind the big vase), with colonies in Western Turkey (Ionia), southern Italy (Magna Graecia), and Sicily. They were developing a written language and achieving the social stability that could afford to generate art. This vase is a baby step in that progression. Next, large-scale statues in stone were developed.

▶ *In Rooms 7-14, you'll get a look at some of these giant statues, including...*

Early Greek Statues: Kore and Kouros, c. 700-500 B.C.

Some of the earliest surviving examples of post-Mycenaean Greek art are these life-size and larger-than-life statues of clothed young women (called kore) and naked young men (called kouros). Influenced by ancient statues of Egyptian pharaohs, the earliest of these are big and stiff, with triangular faces and arms at their sides. As you walk through the next few rooms,

The Dipylon vase depicts stick-figure mourners tearing out their hair in grief.

you'll see the statues become more realistic and natural in their movements, with more personality than we see in these earlier rigid shells.

▶ *Facing the vase in the middle of Room 7 is a...*

❻ Female Statue (#1), c. 650 B.C.

With hands at her sides, a skinny figure, a rectangular shape, and dressed in a full-length robe (called a chiton), this kore looks as much like a pillar as a woman. Her lion-mane hairstyle resembles an Egyptian headdress. The writing down her left leg says she's dedicated to Apollo. Stroll around. The Egyptian influence is clear.

▶ *In the next room (Room 8), your eyes go right to a very nice pair of knees that belong to a...*

❼ Kouros from Sounion (#2720), c. 600 B.C.

A typical kouros from the Archaic Period (c. 800-500 B.C.), this young naked man has braided dreadlocks and a stable forward-facing pose, and is stepping forward slightly with his left leg. His fists are clenched at his sides, and his scarred face obscures an Archaic smile—a placid smile that suggests the inner secret of happiness. His anatomy is strongly geometrical and stylized, with almond-shaped eyes, oval pecs, an arched ribcage, cylindrical thighs, and a too-perfect symmetry. The overdeveloped muscles (look at those quads!) and his narrow waist resemble those of an athletic teenager.

Rather than strict realism, kouros statues capture a geometric ideal. The proportions of the body parts follow strict rules—for example, most statues are precisely seven "heads" tall. Although this kouros steps forward slightly, his hips remain even (think about it—the hips of a real person would shift forward on one side). The Greeks were obsessed with the human body, and remember, these statues were of humans, not gods. Standing naked and alone, these statues represented a microcosm of the rational order of nature.

Statues were painted in vivid, lifelike colors. Notice that the rough surface of the marble lacks the translucent sheen of Classical Age statues (Archaic chisels were not yet strong or efficient enough to avoid shattering the crystalline marble).

Kouros statues were everywhere, presented as gifts to a god at a temple or to honor the dead in a cemetery. This one was dedicated to Poseidon at the entrance to the temple at Sounion. As a funeral figure, a

Left to right: female statue #1, kouros from Sounion, kore with flower, kouros stepping out.

kouros represented the deceased in his prime of youth and happiness, forever young.

▶ *Continue into the next room (Room 11). On the left, holding a flower, is a...*

❽ Statue of a Kore (#4889), c. 550 B.C.

Where a male kouros was either life-size or larger than life and naked (emphasizing masculine power), a female kore was often slightly smaller than life and modestly clothed, capturing feminine grace. This petite kore stands with feet together, wearing a pleated chiton belted at the waist. Her hair is braided and held in place with a wreath, and she wears a necklace. Her right hand tugs at her dress, indicating motion (a nice trick if the artist lacks the skill to actually show it), while her left hand holds a flower. Like most ancient statues, she was painted in lifelike colors, including her skin. Her dress was red—you can still see traces of the paint—adorned with flower

The Four Stages of Greek Sculpture

Archaic (c. 700-480 B.C.): Rigid statues with stylized anatomy, facing forward, with braided hair and mysterious smiles (see photo at right).

Severe (c. 480-460 B.C.): More realistic and balanced statues (with no smiles), capturing a serious nobility.

Classical (c. 460-323 B.C.): Realistic statues whose poses strike a balance between movement and stillness, with understated emotion. (Within this period, the Golden Age was roughly 450-400 B.C.)

Hellenistic (c. 323-30 B.C.): Photorealistic (even ugly) humans engaged in dramatic, emotional struggles, captured in snapshot poses that can be wildly unbalanced.

designs and a band of swastikas down the front. (In ancient times—before German archaeologist Schliemann's writings popularized it and Hitler appropriated it—the swastika was a harmless good-luck symbol representing the rays of the sun.) This kore, like all the statues in the room, has that distinct Archaic smile (or smirk, as the Greeks describe it).

▶ *The next room—a long hall labeled Room 13—has...*

❾ More Kouroi and Bases for Funerary Kouroi (#3476 and #3477)

These statues, from the late Archaic Period (around 500 B.C.), once decorated the tombs of hero athletes—perhaps famous Olympians. Notice that these young men are slightly more relaxed and realistic, with better-formed thighs and bent elbows. Some kouros statues stood on pedestals, like the two square marble bases located farther down Room 13 (left side). The indentations atop each base held a kouros statue that represented an idealized version of the deceased. On the first base, the carved relief shows wrestlers and other athletes. Perhaps this was an excuse for the artist to show off a new ability to depict the body in a twisting pose. Notice the cute dog-and-cat fight. The second base features a game of field hockey—each scene reflecting the vigor of the deceased man in his prime.

During the Archaic Period, Greece was prospering, growing, expanding, trading, and colonizing the Mediterranean. The smiles on the statues capture the bliss of a people settling down and living at peace. But in 480 B.C., Persia invaded, and those smiles suddenly vanished.

▶ *Pass through Room 14 and into Room 15, which is dominated by one of the jewels of the collection, the...*

⑩ Bronze Statue of Zeus or Poseidon, Called the Artemision Bronze (#X. 15161), c. 460 B.C.

The god steps forward, raises his arm, sights along his other arm at the distant target, and prepares to hurl his thunderbolt (if it's Zeus) or trident (if Poseidon). This statue was discovered amid a shipwreck off Cape Artemision in 1928. The weapon was never found, so no one knows for sure if this is Zeus or Poseidon.

The god stands 6'10" and has a physique like mine. His hair is curly and tied at the back, and his now-hollow eyes once shone white with inset bone. He plants his left foot and pushes off with the right. Even though every limb moves in a different direction, the whole effect is one of balance. The statue's dimensions are a study in Greek geometry. His head is one Greek foot high, and he's six heads tall (or one Greek fathom). The whole figure has an "X" shape that would fit into a perfect circle, with his navel at the center and his fingertips touching the rim. Although the bronze statue—cast with the "lost wax" technique (explained later, on page 113)—is fully three-dimensional, it's most impressive from the front. Later Greek statues seem fully alive from every angle, including the three-quarter view.

Zeus/Poseidon is an example of the so-called Severe style (500-450 B.C.). Historically, the Severe period covers the time when Greece battled the Persians and emerged victorious—the era when ordinary men shook off tyrants and controlled their own destiny through democracy. The Greeks were entering the dawn of the Golden Age. During this time of horrific war, the Greeks made art that was serious (no more Archaic smiles), unadorned, and expressed the noble strength and heroism of the individuals who had carried them through tough times. The statues are anatomically realistic, celebrating the human form.

With this statue of Zeus/Poseidon, his movements frozen in time, we can examine the wonder of the physical body. He's natural yet ideal, twisting yet balanced, moving while at rest. With his geometrical perfection and godlike air, the figure sums up all that is best about the art of the ancient world.

The 6'10" bronze god is frozen at the exact moment he's set to hurl his weapon.

▶ *Next, we enter the Golden Age. Room 16 is filled with big, tall vases made of marble, labeled* **⓫ Attic Funerary Monuments.** *These gravestones are in the shape of actual ceramic urns used as coffins to bury people in ancient times. (The Greeks also burned their dead on open biers.)*

Continue through Room 16 and into Room 17. The WCs and café are out the door and downstairs, in the courtyard. From Room 17, turn right into Rooms 19 and 20 (then right again, then left). At the dead-end is a small glass case containing the...

⓬ Statuette of Athena (#129), Called the Athena Varvakeion, c. A.D. 250, Original from 438 B.C.

This is the most famous copy of the statue of *Athena Varvakeion* by Pheidias—a one-twelfth-size replica of the 40-foot statue that once stood in the Parthenon (c. 438 B.C.). Though just a miniature copy of the glorious original, it provides a good look at Greek art at its Golden Age pinnacle. Athena stands dressed in flowing robes, holding a small figure of Nike (goddess of victory) in her right hand and a shield in her left. Athena's helmet sprouts plumes with winged horses and a sphinx. To give a sense of scale of the original, the tiny Nike in Athena's hand was six feet tall in the Parthenon statue. Athena loved snakes, which shed their skin, representing renewal. There's a big one next to her shield, she wears a snake belt and bracelet, coiled snakes decorate her breastplate, and the snake-headed Medusa (whom Athena helped Perseus slay) adorns the center of her chest. (For more on the statue's original location, see page 60.)

▶ *Backtrack to Room 17, turn right, and continue circling the museum clockwise into room 18, which has....*

Small-scale version of 40-foot Athena.

Funeral stele—a mother mourns her baby.

⓭ Funeral Steles

The tombstones that fill this room, all from the fifth century B.C., are more good examples of Golden Age Greek art. With a mastery of the body, artists show poignant scenes of farewell, as loved ones bid a sad good-bye to the dead, who are seated. While the dead are often just shaking hands, there's usually a personal meaning with each scene. On the tombstone opposite the window, a woman who died in childbirth looks at her baby, held by a servant as it reaches for its dead mother. Other scenes include a beautiful young woman who died in her prime, narcissistically gazing into a mirror. Servants are shown taking part in the sad event, as if considered part of the family. In the center of the room, a rich and powerful woman ponders which treasure from her jewel box to take with her into eternity. While shallow reliefs, these works are effectively three-dimensional. There's a timeless melancholy in the room, a sense that no matter who you are—or how powerful or affluent your family is—when you go, you go alone...and shrouds have no pockets.

▶ *Pass into Room 21, a large central hall. We'll take a temporary break from the chronological sequence to see statues dating from the second century B.C., when Greece was ruled by Rome. The hall is dominated by the...*

⓮ Bronze Statue of a Horse and Jockey of Artemision (#X.15177), c. 140 B.C.

The horse is in full stride, and the young jockey looks over his shoulder to see if anyone's gaining on them. In his left hand he holds the (missing) reins, while with his right he whips the horse to go even faster—maybe too fast, judging by the look on his face.

Greeks loved their horse races, and this statue may celebrate a victory at one of the Panhellenic Games. The jockey (who has the features of a non-Greek) is dressed in a traditional short tunic, has inlaid eyes, and was originally painted black—probably depicting a mixed-race Ethiopian.

The statue, like other ancient bronzes done by Greeks in Roman times, was made not by hammering sheets of metal, but with the classic "lost wax" technique. The artist would first make a rough version of the statue out of clay, cover it with a layer of wax, and then cover that with another layer of clay to make a form-fitting mold. When heated in a furnace to harden the mold, the wax would melt—or be "lost"—leaving a narrow

Horse and jockey—unbridled emotion.

Realistic grave relief.

space between the clay model and the mold. The artist would then pour molten bronze into the space, let it cool, break the mold, and—*voilà!*—end up with a hollow bronze statue. This particular statue was cast in pieces, which were then welded together. After the cast was removed, the artist added a few surface details and polished it smooth. Notice the delightful detail on the rider's spurs, which were lashed to his bare feet.

Stylistically, we've gone from stiff Archaic, to restrained Severe, to balanced Classical...to this preview of the unbridled emotion of Hellenism.

The other statues in the room are second-century B.C. Roman copies of fifth-century B.C. Greek originals. While the Romans were great warriors, engineers, and administrators, they had an inferiority complex when it came to art and high culture. For high-class Romans, Greek culture was the ideal, which created a huge demand for Greek statues. As demand exceeded supply, making copies of Greek originals became a big industry, and the Romans excelled at it. In fact, throughout Europe today, when you see a "Greek" statue, it's likely a Roman copy of a Greek original. Thanks to excellent copies like the ones in this room, we know what many (otherwise lost) Golden Age Greek masterpieces looked like.

▶ *To return to our chronological tour (picking up back before the Romans arrived), head into Room 22, with pediment reliefs (Sack of Troy on the right, Greeks vs. Amazons on the left) that once decorated the Temple of Asklepios at Epidavros. Pass through a couple of rooms displaying funeral monuments with progressively higher relief and more monumental scale until you reach the long Room 28, where you'll come face-to-face with a large...*

⓯ Grave Relief of a Horse (#4464), Late Fourth Century B.C.

The spirited horse steps lively and whinnies while an Ethiopian boy struggles with the bridle and tries to calm him with food. The realistic detail of the horse's muscles and veins is astonishing, offset by the panther-skin blanket. The horse's head pops out of the relief, becoming fully three-dimensional. The boy's pose is slightly off-balance, anticipating the "un-posed poses" of later Hellenism. We sense the emotions of both the overmatched boy and the nervous horse. We also see a balance between the horse and boy, with the two figures creating a natural scene together rather than standing alone.

▶ *Farther down Room 28 stands the impressive, slightly-larger-than-life-size...*

⓰ Bronze Statue of a Youth (#X.13396), c. 340-330 B.C.

Scholars can't decide if this statue is reaching out to give someone an apple or demonstrating a split-finger fastball. He's most likely the mythical Paris, awarding a golden apple to the winner of a beauty contest between goddesses (sparking jealousies that started the Trojan War).

The statue is caught in mid-step as he reaches out, gazing intently at the person he's giving the object to. Split this youth vertically down the middle to see the *contrapposto* (or "counter-poise") stance of so many Classical statues. His left foot is stable, while the right moves slightly, causing his hips to shift. His right arm is tense while the left hangs loose. These subtle, contrary motions are in perfect balance around the statue's vertical axis.

In the Classical Age, statues reached their peak of natural realism and balanced grace. During the following Hellenistic Period, sculptors added to that realism, injecting motion and drama. Statues are fully three-dimensional, interesting from every angle. Their poses are less rigid than those in the Archaic Period and less overtly heroic than those of the Severe. The beauty of the face, the perfection of the muscles, the balance of elegant grace and brute power—these represent the full ripeness of the art of this age.

▶ *Continue into the small Room 29. To the left of the following door, find a black bronze head in a glass case. Look into the wild and cynical inlaid eyes of this...*

Bronze youth—perfectly balanced grace.

Philosopher, a Hellenist individual.

⑰ Portrait Head from a Statue of a Philosopher (#X.13400), c. 240 B.C.

This philosopher was a Cynic, part of a movement of non-materialist nonconformists founded in the fourth century B.C. by Diogenes. The term "cynic" aptly describes these dislikable, arrogant guys with unkempt hair. The statue's aged, bearded face captures the personality of a distinct individual. It's typical of the Hellenistic Period, the time after the Macedonian Alexander the Great conquered Greece and proceeded to spread Greek values across much of the Mediterranean and beyond. Hellenistic Greek society promoted a Me-Generation individualism, and artists celebrated everyday people like this. For the first time in history, we see human beings in all their gritty human glory: with wrinkles, male-pattern baldness, saggy boobs, and middle-age spread, all captured in less-than-noble poses.

This head, like a number of the museum's statues, was found by archaeologists on the seabed off the coast of Greece. Two separate shipwrecks in ancient times have yielded treasures now in this museum: At the wreck off Cape Artemision (north of Athens), Zeus/Poseidon and the *Horse and Jockey* were found. Another wreck, off the tiny island of Antikythira (near the southern tip of the Peloponnesian Peninsula), is the source of this statue, as well as the *Bronze Statue of a Youth* and the Antikythira Mechanism (a crude computer from the first century B.C.—it's in Room 38).

▶ *Continue into the long Room 30 and head to the far end to find the...*

⑱ Statue of a Fighting Gaul (#247), c. 100 B.C.

Having been wounded in the thigh (note the hole), this soldier has fallen to one knee and reaches up to fend off the next blow. The helmet indicates that he's not a Greek, but a Gaul from Galatia (western Turkey). The artist catches the exact moment when the tide of battle is about to turn. The face of this Fighting Gaul says he's afraid he may become the Dying Gaul.

The statue sums up many of the features of Hellenistic art: He's frozen in motion, in a wild, unbalanced pose that dramatizes his inner thoughts. The diagonal pose runs up his left leg and out his head and outstretched arm. Rather than a noble, idealized god, this is an ordinary soldier caught in an extreme moment. His arms flail, his muscles strain, his eyes bulge, and he cries out in pain. This statue may have been paired with others, creating a theatrical mini-drama that heightens the emotion. Hellenism shows us the thrill of victory, and—in this case—the agony of defeat.

▶ *Directly to the right is a...*

⑲ Statue of Aphrodite, Pan, and Eros (#3335)

In this playful ensemble from the sacred island of Delos, Aphrodite—seen here in a rare total nude of a female—is about to whack Pan with her sandal. Striking a classic *contrapposto* pose (with most of her weight on one foot), Aphrodite is more revealing than modest, her voluptuous body polished smooth. There's a bit of whimsy here, as Aphrodite seems to be saying: "Don't! Stop!"...but may instead be saying: "Don't stop." The actions of the (literally) horny Pan can also be interpreted in two ways: His left arm is forceful, but his right is gentle—holding her more like a dance partner. Eros, like an omnipresent Tinkerbell, comes to Aphrodite's aid—or does he? He has the power to save her if she wants help, but with a hand on Pan's horn and a wink, Eros seems to say: "OK, Pan, this is your chance. Come on, man, go for it." Pan can't believe his luck. This marble is finer than those used in earlier statues, and it has been polished to a sheen with an emery stone. As you walk around this delightful statue, enjoy the detail,

Fighting Gaul with unbalanced pose.

Aphrodite, Pan, and Eros flirting.

from the pudgy baby feet and the remnants of red paint on the sandal to the way the figures all work together in a cohesive vignette.

▶ *Enter Room 31.*

⓴ Statue of the Emperor Augustus (#X.23322), c. 12-10 B.C.

The Roman emperor rides commandingly atop a (missing) horse, holding the (missing) reins in his left hand. Although Greece was conquered by the Romans (146 B.C.), Greek culture ultimately "conquered" the Romans, as the Grecophile Romans imported Greek statues to Italy to beautify their villas. They preserved Greece's monuments and cranked out high-quality copies of Greek art. When the Roman Emperor Augustus began remaking the city of Rome, he used Greek-style Corinthian columns—a veneer of sophistication on buildings erected with no-nonsense, brick-and-concrete Roman-arch engineering. It's largely thanks to the Romans and their respect for Greek culture that so much of this ancient art survives today.

Emperor Augustus and the Romans conquered Greece, but they succumbed to Greek culture.

Sights

Compared to Europe's other big cities, Athens is relatively light on things to do and see. But the few major sights it does have are big-time. This chapter lists worthwhile sights in Athens, arranged by neighborhood. The biggies—the Acropolis, Ancient Agora, Acropolis Museum, and National Archaeological Museum—are described in much more detail in their individual chapters. There you'll find self-guided tours, plus tips on how to avoid lines, save money, and get a decent bite to eat nearby. Other attractions, including churches and less-prominent ancient sights, are also covered in greater depth in my Athens City Walk. If there's more information on a sight elsewhere, it's marked with a ✪.

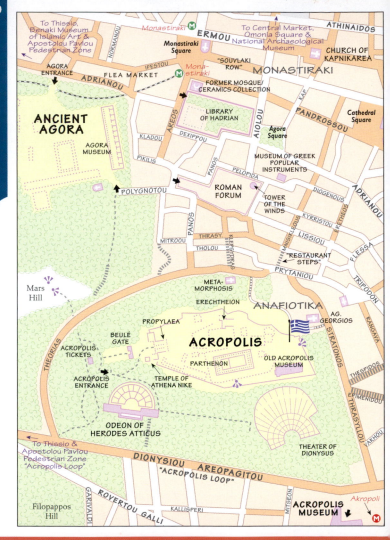

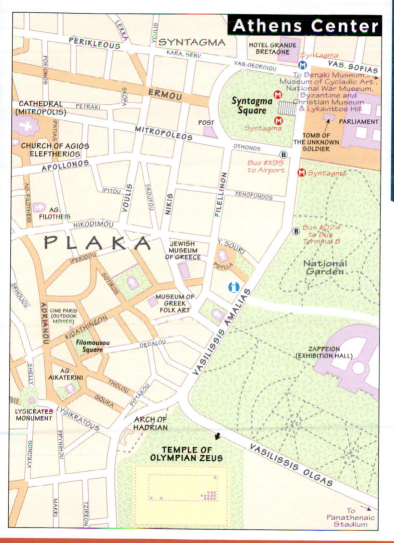

Athens Center

PERIKLEOUS
SYNTAGMA
LEKKA
STILIS
KARA. SERV.
FOKIONOS

HOTEL GRANDE
BRETAGNE
Syntagma
VAS. SOFIAS

ERMOU
SKOPA
VAS.GEORGIOU

CATHEDRAL
(MITROPOLIS)
PETRAKI

To Benaki Museum,
Museum of Cycladic Art,
National War Museum,
Byzantine and
Christian Museum
& Lykavittos Hill

Syntagma
Square

IPATIAS
MITROPOLEOS
POST
Syntagma
PARLIAMENT

CHURCH OF AGIOS
ELEFTHERIOS
APOLLONOS
OTHONOS
TOMB OF
THE UNKNOWN
SOLDIER

AG. FILOTHEIS
IPITOU
VOULIS
SKOUFOU
NIKIS
Bus #X95
to Airport
Syntagma

AG.
FILOTHEIS
NIKODIMOU
XENOFONDOS

P L A K A
JEWISH
MUSEUM
OF GREECE
Y. SOURI
Bus #024
to Bus
Terminal B

IPERIDOU
PSYLLA
National
Garden

SKOULOU
SOTIROS
MUSEUM OF
GREEK
FOLK ART

ADRIANOU
CINE PARIS
(OUTDOOR
MOVIES)
KIDATHINEON
Filomousou
Square
DEDALOU

SHELLY
AG.
AIKATERINI
THOLOU
PITTAKOU
GOURA
VASILISSIS AMALIAS
ZAPPEION
(EXHIBITION HALL)

LYSICRATES
MONUMENT
LYSIKRATOUS
ARCH OF
HADRIAN

SONDZXLA
FRYNIHOU
MAKRI
TZIREON
TEMPLE OF
OLYMPIAN ZEUS
VASILISSIS OLGAS

To
Panathenaic
Stadium

Sights

ACROPOLIS AND NEARBY

A broad pedestrian boulevard that I call the "Acropolis Loop" strings together the Acropolis, Mars Hill, Theater of Dionysus, Acropolis Museum, and more.

▲▲▲ Acropolis

The most important ancient sights in the Western world, the Acropolis ("high city") is where the Greeks built the mighty Parthenon—the most famous temple on the planet and an enduring symbol of ancient Athens' glorious Golden Age.

⭐ See the Acropolis Tour chapter.

▲▲ "Acropolis Loop"

One of Athens' best attractions, this wide, well-manicured, delightfully traffic-free pedestrian boulevard circles the Acropolis. It's composed of two streets with tongue-twisting names—Dionysiou Areopagitou and Apostolou Pavlou (think of them as Dionysus Street and Apostle Paul's Street); for simplicity, I refer to them collectively as the "Acropolis Loop." One of the city's many big improvements made in preparation for its 2004 Olympics-hosting bid, this walkway immediately became a favorite hangout, with vendors, al fresco cafés, and frequent special events enlivening its cobbles.

Dionysiou Areopagitou, wide and touristy, runs along the southern base of the Acropolis. It was named for Dionysus the Areopagite, a member of the ancient Roman-era senate that met atop Mars Hill (described next). The other section, **Apostolou Pavlou**—quieter, narrower, and tree-lined—curls around the western end of the Acropolis and the Ancient Agora. It feels more local and has the best concentration of outdoor eateries (in the Thissio neighborhood). This section was named for the Apostle Paul, who presented himself before Dionysus the Areopagite at Mars Hill.

▲ Mars Hill (Areopagus)

The knobby, windswept hill crawling with tourists in front of the Acropolis is Mars Hill, also known as Areopagus (from *Areios Pagos,* "Ares Hill," referring to the Greek version of Mars). While the views from the Acropolis are more striking, rugged Mars Hill (near the Acropolis' main entrance, at the

Acropolis Ticket

Your €12 Acropolis ticket covers entry to Athens' major ancient sights, including the Acropolis, Ancient Agora, Roman Forum, Temple of Olympian Zeus, Library of Hadrian, and Theater of Dionysus. If you see only the Acropolis, you'll still pay €12—so the other sites are effectively free. (The other attractions do sell cheaper individual tickets—but as you're virtually guaranteed to visit the Acropolis sometime during your trip, these are pointless.) It's technically valid for four days, but there's no date printed on the ticket, so in practice you can use it anytime. The ticket is one long strip; perforated "coupons" are removed and used to enter the smaller sites. You can buy the ticket at any participating site. Only the Acropolis ticket is unique—the other stubs can be used as you like.

western end) makes a pleasant perch. As you're climbing Mars Hill, be warned: The stone stairs (and the top of the rock) have been polished to a slippery shine by history, and can be treacherous even when dry. Watch your step and use the metal staircase.

This hill has an interesting history. After Rome conquered Athens in 86 B.C., the Roman overlords wisely decided to extend citizenship to any free man born here. (The feisty Greeks were less likely to rise up against a state that had made them citizens.) While Rome called the shots on major issues, minor matters of local governance were determined on this hill by a gathering of leaders. During this time, the Apostle Paul—the first great Christian missionary and author of about half of the New Testament—preached to the Athenians here on Mars Hill. Paul looked out over the Agora and started talking about an altar he'd seen—presumably in the Agora (though archaeologists can't confirm)—to the "Unknown God." (A plaque embedded in the rock near the stairs contains the Greek text of Paul's speech.) Although the Athenians were famously open-minded, Paul encountered a skeptical audience and only netted a couple of converts (including Dionysus the Areopagite, a local judge and the namesake of the pedestrian drag behind the Acropolis). Paul moved on to Corinth and a better reception.

Theater of Dionysus

The very scant remains of this theater are scattered southeast of the Acropolis, just above the Dionysiou Areopagitou walkway. It's fair to say that this is where our culture's great tradition of theater was born. During Athens' Golden Age, Sophocles and others watched their plays performed here. Originally just grass, with a circular dirt area as the stage, the theater was eventually expanded to accommodate 17,000—and stone seating was added—in 342-326 B.C., during the time of Alexander the Great. Later the Romans added a raised stage. During Roman times, the theater was connected to the Odeon of Herodes Atticus (see page 48) by a long, covered stoa, creating an ensemble of inviting venues.

▶ *€2, covered by Acropolis ticket, same hours as Acropolis, main gate across from Acropolis Museum, tel. 210-322-4625.*

▲▲▲Acropolis Museum

Located at the foot of Athens' famous ancient hill, this modern-day temple to the Acropolis contains relics from Greece's most famous sight.

⭐ See the Acropolis Museum Tour chapter.

ANCIENT AGORA AND BEYOND

▲▲▲Ancient Agora: Athens' Market

Although literally and figuratively overshadowed by the impressive Acropolis, the Agora was for eight centuries the true meeting place of the city—a hive of commerce, politics, and everyday bustle.

⭐ See the Ancient Agora Tour chapter.

Remains of the Theater of Dionysus.

Great nightlife and views in Thissio.

▲▲Thissio and Psyrri

These two neighborhoods, just west and north (respectively) of the Ancient Agora, offer a real-world alternative to the tourist-clogged, artificial-feeling Plaka. **Thissio,** around the far side of the Acropolis (just follow the main pedestrian drag) has a trendy, yuppie vibe and a thriving passel of cafés and restaurants with point-blank Acropolis views. **Psyrri**—the yang to Thissio's yin—is grungy and run-down, but increasingly populated by a wide range of eateries, cafés, and clubs, with everything from dives to exclusive dance halls to crank-'em-out chain restaurants. While enjoyable any time of day, both neighborhoods are ideal in the evening—either for dinner or for a stroll afterwards. Both also have appealing open-air cinemas (see page 170).

Benaki Museum of Islamic Art

Sometimes it seems the Greeks would rather just forget the Ottoman chapter of their past...but when you're talking about nearly 400 years, that's difficult to do. If you're intrigued by what Greeks consider a low point in their history, pay a visit to this branch of the prominent, private Benaki Museum (see listing for main branch on page 130). The 8,000-piece collection, displayed in two renovated Neoclassical buildings, includes beautifully painted ceramics, a 10th-century golden belt, a rare 14th-century astrolabe, and an entire marble room from a 17th-century Cairo mansion.

▶ *€7, free entry on Wed, Tue-Sun 9:00-15:00, Wed until 21:00, closed Mon, Agion Asomaton 22, on the corner with Dipilou, Metro line 1/green: Thissio, tel. 210-325-1311, www.benaki.gr.*

IN SYNTAGMA

These three sights are covered in more detail in the ✪ Athens City Walk chapter.

▲Syntagma Square (Plateia Syntagmatos)

The "Times Square" of Athens is named for Greece's historic 1843 constitution, prompted by demonstrations right on this square. A major transit hub, the square is watched over by Neoclassical masterpieces such as the Hotel Grande Bretagne and the Parliament building.

Parliament

The former palace of King Otto, this is now a house of democracy. In front, colorfully costumed evzone guards stand at attention at the Tomb of the Unknown Soldier and periodically do a ceremonial changing of the guard to the delight of tourists. Guards change five minutes before the top of each hour, with a less elaborate crossing of the guard on the half-hour and a full ceremony with marching band most Sundays at 11:00.

Ermou Street

This pedestrianized thoroughfare, connecting Syntagma Square with Monastiraki (and on to Thissio), is packed with top-quality international shops. While most Athenians can't afford to shop here, it's enjoyable for people-watching and is refreshingly traffic-free in an otherwise congested area.

CHURCHES IN THE PLAKA

All of these sights are covered in detail in the ⭐ Athens City Walk chapter. Only the basics are listed here.

▲Church of Kapnikarea

Sitting unassumingly in the middle of Ermou street, this small, typical, 11th-century Byzantine church offers a convenient look at the Greek Orthodox faith.

▶ *Free, likely open daily 8:30-13:30 & 17:00-19:30.*

▲Cathedral (Mitropolis)

Dating from the mid-19th century, this big but stark head church of Athens—and therefore of all of Greece—has been covered in scaffolding inside and out since a 1989 earthquake. The cathedral is the centerpiece of a reverent neighborhood, with a pair of statues out front honoring great heroes of the Church and surrounding streets lined with religious para-phernalia shops (and black-cloaked, long-bearded priests).

▶ *Free, generally open daily 8:00-13:00 & 16:30-20:00, no afternoon clo-sure in summer, Plateia Mitropoleos.*

▲Church of Agios Eleftherios

This tiny church, huddled in the shadow of the cathedral, has a delightful hodgepodge of ancient and early Christian monuments embedded in its facade. Like so many Byzantine churches, it was partly built (in the 13th century) with fragments of earlier buildings, monuments, and even tombstones. Today it's a giant puzzle of millennia-old bits and pieces.

▶ *Free, likely open daily 8:30-13:30 & 17:00-19:30, Plateia Mitropoleos.*

EAST OF THE PLAKA

Busy Vasilissis Amalias rumbles south of Syntagma Square, where you'll find most of the following sights. The first two date from Athens' Roman period and are located at the edge of the tourist zone (just a few steps up Dionysiou Areopagitou from the Acropolis Museum and Metro line 2/red: Akropoli, or a 10-minute walk south of Syntagma Square). Both are described in greater detail in the ✪ Athens City Walk chapter. The National Garden and Zappeion are just north of these sights.

▲Arch of Hadrian

This stoic triumphal arch marks the entrance to what was once the proud "Hadrianopolis" development—a new suburb of ancient Athens built by the Roman Emperor Hadrian in the second century A.D. Just beyond the arch is the Temple of Olympian Zeus.

▶ *Free, always viewable.*

▲▲Temple of Olympian Zeus

Started by an overambitious tyrant in the sixth century B.C., this giant temple was not completed until Hadrian took over, seven centuries later. Now 15 (of the original 104) Corinthian columns stand evocatively over a ruined base in a field. You can get a good view of the temple ruins through the fence by the Arch of Hadrian, but since it's covered by the Acropolis ticket, you can easily drop in for a closer look.

▶ *€2, covered by Acropolis ticket, daily 8:00-20:00, Sept until 19:00, off-season until 17:00, tel. 210-922-6330, www.culture.gr.*

National Garden

Extending south from the Parliament, the National Garden is a wonderfully cool retreat from the traffic-clogged streets of central Athens. Covering an area of around 40 acres, it was planted in 1839 as the palace garden, created for the pleasure of Queen Amalia. The garden was opened to the public in 1923.

▶ *Free, open daily from dawn to dusk.*

Zappeion

At the southern end of the National Garden, this grand mansion (now a conference and exhibition center) is surrounded by formal gardens of its own. To most Athenians, the Zappeion is best known as the site of the Aigli Village outdoor cinema in summer (behind the building, on the right as you face the colonnaded main entry; see page 171). But the building is more than just a backdrop. During Ottoman rule, much of the Greek elite, intelligentsia, and aristocracy fled the country. They returned after independence and built grand mansions such as this. Finished in 1888, it was designed by the Danish architect Theophilus Hansen, who was known (along with his brother Christian) for his Neoclassical designs. The financing was provided by the Zappas brothers, Evangelos and Konstantinos, two of the prime movers in the campaign to revive the Olympic Games. This mansion housed the International Olympic Committee during the first modern Olympics in 1896 and served as a media center during the 2004 Olympics.

▶ *Gardens free and always open, building only open during exhibitions for a fee, Vasilissis Amalias, Metro line 2/red: Akropoli or line 3/blue: Evangelismos, tel. 210-323-7830.*

▲Panathenaic (a.k.a. "Olympic") Stadium

Here's your chance to see an intact ancient stadium. This gleaming marble stadium has many names. Officially it's the Panathenaic Stadium, built in the fourth century B.C. to host the Panathenaic Games. Sometimes it's referred to as the Roman Stadium, because it was rebuilt by the great Roman benefactor Herodes Atticus in the second century A.D., using the same prized Pentelic marble that was used in the Parthenon. This magnificent white marble gives the place its most popular name: Kalimarmara ("Beautiful Marble") Stadium. It was restored to its Roman condition in preparation for the first modern Olympics in 1896. It saw Olympic action again in 2004, when it provided a grand finish for the marathon. In ancient times, 50,000 filled the stadium; today, 80,000 people can pack the stands.

▶ *€3, daily March-Oct 8:00-19:00, Nov-Feb 8:00-17:00, southeast of the Zappeion off Vasileos Konstantinou, Metro line 2/red: Akropoli or line 3/ blue: Evangelismos, tel. 210-325-1744, www.panathenaicstadium.gr.*

NORTH OF MONASTIRAKI

Athinas street leads north from Monastiraki Square to Omonia Square. Walking this grand street offers a great chance to feel the pulse of modern, workaday Athens, with shops tumbling onto broad sidewalks, striking squares, nine-to-fivers out having a smoke, and lots of urban energy. The first two sights are on the way to Omonia Square. Farther up Athinas street, past Omonia Square, is the National Archaeological Museum.

Central Market

Take a vibrant, fragrant stroll through the modern-day version of the Ancient Agora. It's a living, breathing, smelly, and (for some) nauseating barrage on all the senses. You'll see dripping-fresh meat, livestock in all stages of dismemberment, still-wriggling fish, exotic nuts, and sticky figs. While it's not Europe's most colorful or appealing market, it offers a lively contrast to Athens' ancient sights.

The entire market square is a delight to explore, with colorful and dirt-cheap souvlaki shops and a carnival of people-watching. The best and cheapest selection of whatever's in season is at the fruit and vegetable stalls, which spread across Athinas street downhill to the west, flanked by shops selling feta from the barrel and a dozen different kinds of olives. Meat and fish markets are housed in the Neoclassical building to the east, behind a row of shops facing Athinas street that specialize in dried fruit and nuts. Try the roasted almonds and the delicious white figs from the island of Evia.

▶ *Open Mon-Sat 7:00-15:00, closed Sun, on Athinas between Sofokleous and Evripidou, between Metro lines 1/green and 2/red: Omonia and Metro lines 1/green and 3/blue: Monastiraki.*

Art Tower

This contemporary gallery is worth seeking out for fans of cutting-edge art. Various temporary exhibits fill some of this skyscraper's eight stimulating floors; if it's open, just poke around. Located near the Central Market action, it's squeezed between produce stalls, overlooking the big, open square with the underground parking garage.

▶ *Free, Wed-Fri 15:00-20:00, Sat 12:00-16:00, closed Sun-Tue, Armodiou 10—look for ΑΡΜΟΔΙΟΥ 10, tel. 210-324-6100, www.artower.gr.*

▲▲▲National Archaeological Museum

This museum is the single best place on earth to see ancient Greek artifacts, from 7,000 B.C. to A.D. 500.

⭐ See National Archaeological Museum Tour chapter.

IN KOLONAKI, EAST OF SYNTAGMA SQUARE

Once the terrain of high-society bigwigs eager to live close to the Royal Palace (now the Parliament), Kolonaki is today's diplomatic quarter. Lining the major boulevard called Vasilissis Sofias are many embassies, a thriving yuppie scene, and some of Athens' top museums outside the old center. These are listed in the order you'd reach them, heading east from the Parliament.

▲▲Benaki Museum of Greek History and Culture

This exquisite collection takes you on a fascinating walk through the ages, from the Neolithic Age to the 20th century. The mind-boggling array of artifacts is crammed into 36 galleries on four floors, covering seemingly every era of history: antiquity, Byzantine, Ottoman, and modern. The private collection nicely complements the many state-run museums in town. Each item is labeled in English, and it's all air-conditioned. The Benaki gift shop is a fine place to buy jewelry (replicas of museum pieces).

You'll see fine painted vases, gold wreaths of myrtle leaves worn on heads 2,300 years ago, and evocative Byzantine icons and jewelry, as well as traditional costumes, furniture, and household items from the period of Ottoman occupation. A fascinating exhibit shows Greece through the eyes of foreign visitors, who came here in the 18th and 19th centuries (back when Athens was still a village, spiny with Ottoman minarets) to see the same ruins you're enjoying today. On the top floor, Romantic art depicts Greece's stirring and successful 19th-century struggle for independence.

▶ €7, free entry on Thu, Wed-Sat 9:00-17:00, Thu until 24:00, Sun 9:00-15:00, closed Mon-Tue, classy rooftop café, across from back corner of National Garden at Koumbari 1, Metro lines 2/red and 3/blue: Syntagma, tel. 210-367-1000, www.benaki.gr.

Other Branches: The Benaki has two other branches scattered around Athens, including the Benaki Museum of Islamic Art (see page 126) and the Benaki Cultural Center (a.k.a. "Pireos Street Annex"), which hosts temporary exhibits with a more modern/contemporary flavor (€3-10 depending on exhibits, Wed-Sun 10:00-18:00, Fri-Sat until 22:00, closed Mon-Tue, at Pireos 138, Metro line 3/blue: Keramikos, tel. 210-345-3111, www.benaki.gr).

▲▲Museum of Cycladic Art

This modern, cozy museum shows off the largest exhibit of Cycladic art anywhere, collected by one of Greece's richest shipping families (the Goulandris clan). You'll get a good first taste of Cycladic art in the National Archaeological Museum; if you're intrigued, come here for more. The exhibition rooms are small, but everything is well-described in English.

The museum's headliner is a collection of fertility figurines from the Cycladic Islands (surrounding the isle of Delos, off the coast southeast of Athens). Though they come in all different sizes, the figurines follow the same general pattern: skinny, standing ramrod-straight, with large alien-like heads.

An engrossing exhibit on the top floor features engaging illustrations, vivid English descriptions, interesting videos, and actual artifacts that resurrect a fun cross-section of the fascinating and sometimes bizarre practices of the ancients: weddings, athletics, agora culture, warfare, and various female- and male-only activities (such as the male-bonding/dining ritual called the symposium).

▶ €7, €3.50 on Mon; Mon and Wed-Sat 10:00-17:00, Thu until 20:00, Sun 11:00-17:00, closed Tue and many religious holidays; Neophytou Douka 4, Metro line 3/blue: Evangelismos; the museum's entrance is a few steps up the side street (Neophytou Douka), while the more prominent corner building, fronting Vasilissis Sofias, is their larger annex (or "New Wing"), hosting special exhibits; tel. 210-722-8321, www.cycladic.gr.

▲▲Byzantine and Christian Museum

This excellent museum traces a rich and often-overlooked chapter of the Greek story: the Byzantine Empire, from Emperor Constantine's move from Rome to Byzantium (which he renamed Constantinople, now known as Istanbul) in A.D. 324 until the fall of Constantinople to the Ottomans in 1453. While the rest of Europe fell into the Dark Ages, Byzantium shone brightly. And, as its dominant language was Greek, today's Greeks proudly consider the Byzantine Empire "theirs." Outside of the Golden Age of antiquity, the Byzantine era is considered the high-water mark for Greek culture.

The permanent exhibit (the building on the left) is organized both chronologically and thematically. Discover how the earliest Byzantine Christians borrowed artistic forms from the Greek and Roman past, and adapted them to fit their emerging beliefs. View mosaics and capitals from the earliest "temples" of Christianity and see how existing ancient temples were "Christianized" for new use. And delve into various facets of Byzantium, including how they administered this vast empire, the use of art in early Christian worship, and the introduction of Western European artistic elements by Frankish and Latin Crusaders during the 13th century.

▶ *€4, Tue-Sun 9:00-16:00, closed Mon; last entry 30 minutes before closing, Vasilissis Sofias 22, Metro line 3/blue: Evangelismos, tel. 210-721-1027, www.byzantinemuseum.gr.*

National War Museum

This imposing three-story museum documents the history of Greek warfare, from Alexander the Great to today. The rabble-rousing exhibit, staffed by members of the Greek armed forces, stirs the soul of a Greek patriot.

The fine Byzantine and Christian Museum.

History and weaponry at the war museum.

Pick up the free booklet as you enter, then ride the elevator upstairs to the first floor. Here you'll get a quick chronological review of Greek military history, including replicas of ancient artifacts you'll see for real in other museums. The mezzanine level focuses on the Greek experience in World War II, including the Nazi occupation, resistance, and liberation. Back on the ground floor, you'll parade past military uniforms, browse an armory of old weapons, and (outside) ogle modern military machines—tanks, fighter jets, and more.

▶ €2, Tue-Sat 9:00-14:00, Sun 9:30-14:00, closed Mon, scant English descriptions but audioguide available, Rizari 2-4 at Vasilissis Sofias, Metro line 3/blue: Evangelismos, tel. 210-725-2975, www.warmuseum.gr.

DAY TRIPS FROM ATHENS

The following destinations are doable as side-trips from Athens. But they'll be much more satisfying with an overnight or as part of a longer Greece itinerary. For more information, see my *Rick Steves' Greece: Athens & the Peloponnese* guidebook.

▲▲▲Hydra

In under two hours, you can sail to this glamorous getaway, combining practical convenience with idyllic Greek island ambience. While Hydra (EE-drah) can be done as a long day trip from Athens, it's better to spend two nights (or more) so you can really relax.

One of the island's greatest attractions is its total absence of cars and motorbikes. Sure-footed donkeys—laden with everything from sandbags

Hydra—Greek-isle ambience two hours away.

Delphi's photogenic Sanctuary of Athena.

and bathtubs to bottled water—climb stepped lanes. The island's main town, also called Hydra, is one of Greece's prettiest. Its busy but quaint harbor—bobbing with rustic fishing boats and luxury yachts—is surrounded by a ring of rocky hills and whitewashed homes. From the harbor, zippy water taxis whisk you to isolated beaches and tavernas.

▶ *Getting There: To reach Hydra, take a Hellenic Seaways high-speed hydrofoil ("Flying Dolphin") or catamaran ("Flying Cat"). Boats leave from the port of Piraeus (near central Athens—see page 161) frequently (9/day June-Sept, 4-7/day Oct-May, 1.75 hours; for tickets, visit a travel agency, call, or go online; tel. 210-419-9000, www.hsw.gr). Note that it's wise to book well in advance, especially for summer weekends, and that weather conditions can cause cancellations.*

▲▲Delphi

Outside of Athens, this is the most spectacular of Greece's ancient sights. Long ago, Delphi (dell-FEE) was the home of a prophetess known as the oracle (a.k.a. the Pythia or sibyl), the mouthpiece of Apollo on earth. Pilgrims came from far and wide to seek her advice on everything from affairs of state to wars to matrimonial problems. Delphi's fame grew, and its religious festivals blossomed into the Pythian Games, an athletic contest that was second only to the Olympics. Today visitors can see the archaeological site, containing the ruins of the Sanctuary of Apollo, and the great Delphi Archaeological Museum, where statues and treasures found on the site help bring the ruins to life.

▶ *€6 for archaeological site, €9 combo-ticket includes museum; April-Oct Tue-Sun 8:00-20:00, Mon 8:30-20:00 (museum closes at 15:00); Nov-March daily 8:30-15:00; hours can change without notice, especially off-season—best to visit before 14:00, last entry 20 minutes before closing, some sections prone to sudden closures—call before coming to confirm everything's open, tel. 22650-82312, www.culture.gr.*

Getting There: Buses between Delphi and Athens depart about every two or three hours (roughly 6/day, 3 hours). It's a 20-minute walk to the archaeological site from the bus station (upon arrival, consider buying a return ticket, since buses can fill up). Or join a package tour from Athens, which includes transportation, a guided tour, and lunch (see page 171).

The Peloponnese

The Peloponnese is the large peninsula that hangs from the rest of the Greek mainland by the narrow Isthmus of Corinth. Though you can day-trip to any of these places from Athens, if you have time, it's best to hunker down in Nafplio for two or three nights, using it as a launchpad for your ancient sightseeing.

▲▲Nafplio

Once the capital of a newly independent Greece (19th century), this histori-cally important town is as chic as Athens, without all the graffiti. While the town's glory days have faded, Nafplio retains a certain genteel panache. Walk the narrow and atmospheric back streets, lined with elegant Venetian houses and Neoclassical mansions. Dip into the fine archaeological mu-seum, featuring relics from prehistoric Greece and the Mycenaean civiliza-tion. Or hike up to Palamidi Fortress, one of three Venetian-built castles guarding the harbor (all wonderfully floodlit at night). The best-preserved castle of its kind in Greece, Palamidi towers over the Old Town, protected to the west by steep cliffs that plunge 650 feet to the sea.

▶ **Getting There:** *It's an easy 2.5-hour drive or bus ride from Athens (bus-es run hourly, www.ktel-argolidas.gr).*

▲Epidavros

Nestled in a leafy valley some 18 miles east of Nafplio, Epidavros was once the most famous healing center in the ancient Greek world. Since pilgrims prayed to Asklepios, the god of medicine, for health, a sanctuary was needed, with a temple, altars, and statues to the gods. The sanctuary reached the height of its popularity in the fourth and third centuries B.C.,

Sights

Nafplio—history, atmosphere, and seafood.

Test the acoustics at Epidavros' theater.

when it boasted medical facilities, housing for the sick, mineral baths, a stadium for athletic competitions, and a theater. These days the famous theater is Epidavros' star attraction. Built into the side of a tree-covered hill, it's the finest and best-preserved of all of Greece's ancient theaters—and that's saying something in a country with 132 of them.

▶ *€6, daily late March-Oct 8:00-19:30, off-season until 17:00, museum opens at 12:00 on Mon, tel. 27350-22009, www.culture.gr.*

   Getting There: *From Nafplio, it's a 45-minute drive or bus ride (3/ day). From Athens, buses head to Nafplio, then continue on to Epidavros (3/day, 2.5 hours, might require a transfer in Nafplio, www.ktel-argolidas .gr).*

▲Mycenae

This fortress city atop a hill was the hub of a mighty civilization that dominated the Greek world between 1600 and 1200 B.C., a thousand years before Athens' Golden Age. Today, a visit to Mycenae is a trip back into prehistory to see some of the oldest remains (in Europe) of a complex civilization. The three main attractions are the archaeological ruins, consisting of the hilltop walled city with its grand Lion Gate entrance; a museum housing artifacts that were found here; and the impressive Treasury of Atreus—a huge domed tomb where Mycenae's royalty were buried.

▶ *€8, daily late March-Sept 8:00-20:00, Oct until 18:30, off-season until 17:00; museum opens at 12:00 on Mon and generally may close a half-hour before the rest of the site; off-season hours can change without notice, and sight may close early when slow—call ahead to confirm; tel. 27510-76802 (at Mycenae) or 27520-27502 (in Nafplio), www.culture.gr.*

   Getting There: *It's 45 minutes by car or bus from Nafplio (2/day, confirm that your bus goes to the archaeological site—other buses take you only as far as Fichti, two miles away; www.ktel-argolidas.gr).*

Sleeping

Small, inexpensive hotels in the Plaka and Syntagma area are relatively scarce, listed in all the guidebooks, and filled with other tourists. Be willing to expand your search beyond the old center. I've found several gems in Makrigianni and Koukaki (behind the Acropolis and a short walk from the Plaka). These typically offer better value and a more sedate and authentic (rather than bustling and touristy) experience. I like hotels that are clean, central, a good value, and friendly, with local character and simple facilities that don't cater to American "needs."

Double rooms listed in this book average about €90, ranging from €55 (very simple, toilet and shower down the hall) to €360 (maximum plumbing and more).

A Typical Athens Hotel

A €90 double room in Athens is small by American standards and has one double bed (either queen-sized or slightly narrower) or two twins. Most bathrooms come with just a shower—if you want a bathtub, ask for one when you reserve. Because of Athens' poor plumbing, don't flush toilet paper—use the bathroom wastebasket instead. Rooms generally have a telephone and TV, and may have a safe. Most hotels at this price will have air-conditioning—cheaper places may not.

In general, lower your expectations. In ramshackle Athens, any room less than €85 will likely come with very well-worn bathrooms and furnishings. At least they're clean...or as clean as an old hotel room can be.

A satisfying Greek breakfast with cheese, ham, yogurt, fresh bread, honey, jam, fruit, juice, and coffee or tea is standard and included in hotel prices. The hotel will likely have Internet access, either free or pay-as-you-go. It may be Wi-Fi in your room or a public terminal in the lobby.

Hoteliers can be a great help and source of advice. Most know their city well, and can assist you with everything from public transit and airport connections to finding a good restaurant, launderette, or Internet café. Most staff speak at least enough English to get by.

Hotels are required to set aside a tenth of their rooms for non-smokers. Since hoteliers are obsessive about cleaning out odors, I never bother asking for a non-smoking room, and so far, I have found all my accommodations acceptable. But if your room smells like the Marlboro man slept there, ask to be moved.

Athens is a noisy city, and Athenians like to stay out late. This, plus heavy street traffic, can challenge light sleepers. I've tried to recommend places in quieter areas, but that's not always possible. Many hotels were renovated for the 2004 Olympics, adding "soundproof" doors and windows that can help block out noise. Still, be ready to use earplugs.

Making Reservations

Reserve ahead, especially in summer. Do it by email (the best way), phone, fax, or through the hotel's website. Your hotelier will want to know:

- the type of room you want (e.g., "one double room with bath")

- how many nights ("three nights")

- dates (using European format: "arriving 22/7/12, departing 25/7/12")

Hotel Price Code

$$$ Most rooms are €100 or more.

$$ Most rooms between €70–100.

$ Most rooms €70 or less.

These rates are for a standard double room with bath during high season. Unless otherwise noted, all hotels listed have an elevator, air-conditioning, and Internet access (either free or fee public computer or Wi-Fi), and breakfast is included.

• special needs ("with...twin beds, air-conditioning, quiet, ground floor")

If the hotel requires your credit-card number for a deposit, you can send it by email (I do), but it's safer via phone, fax, or the hotel's secure website. Once your room is booked, print out the confirmation, and call to reconfirm your reservation a day or two in advance. If you must cancel your reservation, some hotels require advance notice or you'll be billed. Even if there's no penalty, it's polite to give at least three days' notice.

Budget Tips

Because of the economic situation in Greece, you'll find good values and soft prices. Some of my listed hotels offer special rates to my readers—it's worth asking when you book your room. To get the best deal, email several hotels to comparison-shop, and check hotel websites for promo deals. You may get a better rate if you offer to pay cash, stay at least three nights, skip breakfast, or simply ask if there are any cheaper rooms. To save money off-season, consider arriving without a reservation and dropping in at the last minute.

You'll pay a premium to stay near the Acropolis. Many hotels have Acropolis-view rooms—some for no extra charge, but usually for a higher rate.

Don't be too cheap when picking a hotel. In summer, pay a little more for air-conditioning. And remember that cheaper places in boring neighborhoods can be depressing. Your Athens experience will be more memorable with a welcoming oasis to call home.

	Price		
PLAKA AND SYNTAGMA NEIGHBORHOODS **Predictable business-class comfort near the old center**			
Hotel Plaka	$$$	Business hotel with rooftop bar/terrace and modern rooms (some with Acropolis views)	
Hotel Hermes	$$$	Same owners as Hotel Plaka, but better value and newer rooms on a quiet street close to Syntagma; RS discount	
Central Hotel	$$$	Sleek rooms with an anonymous vibe; some rooms have balconies and views	
Athens Cypria Hotel	$$$	In a local-feeling shopping zone with character-less but comfortable rooms	
Hotel Grande Bretagne	$$$	Five-star splurge with 19th-century elegance; ranks among the grand hotels of the world	
Hotel Electra Palace	$$$	Luxury hotel in a nondescript urban zone with plush rooms and snooty service; Acropolis-view outdoor pool	
Hotel Acropolis House	$$	Homey villa filled with antiques and dark-wood furnishings, pay in cash, no elevator	
Niki Hotel	$$	New Age hotel with tight-but-trendy rooms and reasonable rates	
Hotel Adonis	$$	On the quiet, traffic-free upper reaches of Kodrou; fourth-floor rooms have good views of the Acropolis	
Pan Hotel	$$	Centrally located, just below Syntagma Square; ancient but well-maintained rooms	
Hotel Kimon	$	Crank-'em-out hotel with well-appointed rooms; no elevator	
Hotel Phaedra	$	Simple but wonderfully located hotel two blocks from Hadrian's Arch; breakfast extra	
Student & Travellers' Inn	$	Plaka's best backpacker hostel, with recently renovated rooms; breakfast extra	
Athens International Youth Hostel (a.k.a. "Hotel Victor Hugo")	$	High-rise hostel just outside the tourist zone near the Metaxourghio Metro stop	

Address/Phone/Website/Email

Kapnikarea 7, tel. 210-322-2096, fax 210-321-1800, www.plakahotel.gr, plaka@tourhotel.gr

Apollonos 19, tel. 210-323-5514, fax 210-321-1800, www.hermeshotel.gr, hermes@tourhotel.gr

Apollonos 21, tel. 210-323-4357, fax 210-322-5244, www.centralhotel.gr, reservation@centralhotel.gr

Diomias 5, tel. 210-323-8034, www.athenscypria.com, info@athenscypria.com

Vassileos Georgiou 1, tel. 210-333-0000, fax 210-322-8034, www.grandebretagne.gr, info.gb@starwoodhotels.com

Nikodimou 18-20, tel. 210-337-0000, fax 210-324-1875, www.electrahotels.gr, salesepath@electrahotels.gr

Kodrou 6-8, tel. 210-322-2344, fax 210-322-6241, www.acropolishouse.gr, htlarchs@otenet.gr

Nikis 27, tel. 210-322-0913, fax 210-322-0886, www.nikihotel.gr, info@nikihotel.gr

Kodrou 3, tel. 210-324-9737, fax 210-323-1602, www.hotel-adonis.gr, info@hotel-adonis.gr

Mitropoleos 11, tel. 210-323-7816, fax 210-323-7819, www.panhotel.gr, reservations@panhotel.gr

Apollonos 27, tel. 210-331-4658, fax 210-321-4203, www.kimonhotelathens.com, info@kimonhotelathens.com

Cherefondos 16, tel. 210-323-8461, fax 210-322-7795, www.hotelphaedra.com, info@hotelphaedra.com

Kidathineon 16, tel. 210-324-4808, fax 210-321-0065, www.studenttravellersinn.com, info@studenttravellersinn.com

16 Victor Hugo, tel. 210-523-2540, www.athens-international.com, info@athens-international.com

	Price		
PSYRRI NEIGHBORHOOD Emerging nightlife and dining district just north of Monastiraki			
Athens Center Square Hotel	$$$	Comfortable home base amid market action; roof garden with Acropolis views; RS discount	
Hotel Cecil	$$	Conveniently located on the edge of Psyrri in a lightly updated old building	
Hotel Attalos	$$	Tired but peaceful budget standby with Acropolis views from roof; breakfast extra	
Hotel Phidias	$	Right on the Apostolou Pavlou pedestrian drag with dated but reasonably priced rooms	
Hotel Tempi	$	On a pedestrian-only street between Syntagma and Monastiraki; no elevator, no breakfast	
MAKRIGIANNI AND KOUKAKI NEIGHBORHOODS Residential area behind the Acropolis			
Hotel Hera	$$$	Great value near the Acropolis, with plush rooms above classy lobby	
Hotel Acropolis Select	$$$	Well-run hotel with can-do staff, generous breakfast, and stylish lobby	
Art Gallery Hotel	$$	Comfy hotel near the top of a pleasant stair-step lane; breakfast extra	
Athens Studios	$$	Well-appointed, good-value apartments with kitchens and nice touches	
Marble House	$	Family-run place with cared-for rooms; breakfast extra, air-con extra, no elevator	
Tony's Hotel	$	Budget option with rooms in two adjacent buildings; breakfast extra, cash only	
Athens Backpackers	$	Youthful and fun-loving, with good bunks and two on-site bars; well-run by gregarious Aussies	

Address/Phone/Website/Email

Aristogitonos 15, reservation tel. 210-322-2706, reception tel. 210-321-1770, www.athenscentersquarehotel.gr, acs@athenshotelsgroup.com

Athinas 39, tel. 210-321-7079, fax 210-321-8005, www.cecil.gr, info@cecil.gr, Trevlakis family

Athinas 29, tel. 210-321-2801, fax 210-324-3124, www.attaloshotel.com, info@attaloshotel.com

Apostolou Pavlou 39, tel. 210-345-9511, fax 210-345-9082, www.phidias.gr, phidiasa@otenet.gr

Aiolou 29, tel. 210-321-3175, fax 210-325-4179, www.tempihotel.gr, info@tempihotel.gr

Falirou 9, tel. 210-923-6682, fax 210-923-8269, www.herahotel.gr, info@herahotel.gr

Falirou 37-39, tel. 210-921-1611, fax 210-921-6938, www.acropoliselect.gr, selective@ath.forthnet.gr

Erecthiou 5, tel. 210-923-8376, fax 210-923-3025, www.artgalleryhotel.gr, artgalleryhotel@gmail.com

Veikou 3A, tel. 210-923-5811, www.athensstudios.gr, info@athensstudios.gr, Edward

Zini 35a, tel. 210-923-4058 or 210-922-8294, fax 210-922-6461, www.marblehouse.gr, info@marblehouse.gr

Zaharitsa 26, tel. 210-923-0561, tel. & fax 210-923-6370, www.hoteltony.gr, tony@hoteltony.gr

Makri 12, tel. 210-922-4044, www.backpackers.gr, info@backpackers.gr

Eating

Greek food is simple...and simply delicious. There's little point in seeking out trendy, non-Greek eateries. Locals and tourists alike fill endless tavernas, *mezedopolios* (eateries selling small plates called *mezedes*), *ouzeries* (bars selling ouzo liquor and pub grub), and other traditional eateries dishing up the basics.

I've listed restaurants by neighborhood (see the maps on pages 154-156). You probably won't be able to resist dining in the Plaka one night, but in that very touristy area, prices are high and quality is mixed. Thissio and Psyrri—very different but equally worthwhile dining zones—are a short walk beyond the Plaka. I've also listed a couple of good options near the Acropolis Museum, in Makrigianni and Koukaki.

Restaurant Price Code

$$$ Most main courses €25 or more.

$$ Most main courses €15-25.

$ Most main courses €15 or less.

Based on the average price of a meat or seafood dish. Salads and *mezes* are several euros cheaper. So a typical meal in a $$ restaurant—including *meze,* main dish, house wine, water, and service—would cost about €40. The circled numbers in the restaurant listings indicate locations on the maps on pages 154-156.

Athenians like to eat late (dinnertime is typically 21:00-24:00). When you sit down, you'll get a basket of bread, often with napkins and flatware tucked inside (a bread and cover charge of €0.50–€1 is standard). Menus are usually in Greek and English—or you can go into the kitchen and point to what you want. The day's specials are sometimes arranged in a display case. Bring cash; credit cards aren't always accepted. For tips on tipping, see page 163. Smoking is banned indoors, so smokers sit outside.

Greek Cuisine

The four Greek food groups are olives (and olive oil), salty feta cheese, tasty tomatoes, and crispy phyllo dough. Virtually every dish is based upon these four building blocks.

Greeks are justly proud of their olive oil: Their country is the third-largest producer in the EU, and they consume almost seven gallons per person a year. Common, edible Greek olives include the purple and almond-shaped *kalamata*; black, wrinkled *throubes*; and large green *halkithiki* (often stuffed).

The best-known Greek cheese is feta, varying from soft, moist, and mild, to sour, hard, and crumbly. Other cheeses include mild, yellow *kasseri* and sweet, nutty *graviera*.

Savory, flaky phyllo-dough pastries called "pies" (*pita,* not to be confused with pita bread) can be starters in restaurants or purchased from a bakery for a tasty bite to go. Look for *spanakopita* (spinach), *tiropita* (cheese), *kreatopita* (lamb), and *meletzanitopita* (eggplant).

Small plates called *meze* (meh-ZAY) are a great way to sample several foods. The most common is Greek salad (a.k.a. *horiatiki,* "village" salad), with chopped tomatoes, rich feta cheese (in a long slab that you break apart with your fork), olives, and onions, all drenched with olive oil. Other typical *mezedes* are *pantzarosalata* (beet salad), *bekri meze* ("drunkard's snack"—chicken, pork, or beef cooked with wine, cloves, cinnamon, and bay leaves), *dolmathes* (grape leaves stuffed with meat or rice), *taramosalata* (fish-roe dip), and *saganaki* (fried cheese).

My favorite snack is souvlaki pita—grilled meat (often pork or chicken) wrapped in pita bread. Souvlaki goes well with *tzatziki,* a thick, garlicky yogurt-and-cucumber sauce. Souvlaki stands are all over Greece. Just order and pay at the cashier, then take your receipt to the counter to claim your meal. Souvlaki places also sell hearty Greek salads and plates of meat shaved from gyros (cooked by stacking meat on a metal skewer and vertically slow-roasting it), along with wine, beer, and ouzo to wash it down.

Eating

Casseroles include the classic moussaka, with layers of minced meat, eggplant, and tomatoes under cheesy béchamel sauce or egg custard; and its meat-and-pasta cousin *pastitsio* ("Greek lasagna"). *Arnaki kleftiko* is slow-cooked lamb wrapped in phyllo dough or parchment paper, while *stifado* is beef stew with onions, tomatoes, cinnamon, and cloves.

Gavros is a seafood appetizer similar to anchovies—drizzle with lemon juice, and eat everything but the little tails. Marinated and grilled octopus is *htapothi;* grilled or fried red mullet is *barbounia. Psari plaki* is fish baked with tomatoes and onions.

For dessert, look for baklava (phyllo dough layered with nuts and honey), *kataifi* (thin phyllo fibers—like shredded wheat—layered with nuts and honey), *ekmek* (custard-/whipped-cream-topped cake made of honey-soaked phyllo fibers), or *loukoumades* (honey-soaked doughnuts).

Water, generally cheap and rarely carbonated, is served in bottles. With dinner, I usually order resin-flavored *retsina* wine, although Greece's non-resinated wine is improving. Beer is mostly imported, but you will find local brands (Alpha, Athenian, Marathon, and Mythos). Cloudy, anise-flavored ouzo is worth a try, and rich, golden-colored Metaxa liqueur is for after dinner.

Starbucks-style coffee houses have invaded Athens, but tavernas still serve traditional Greek coffee, made with loose grounds. In summer, Greeks sip iced coffee drinks, including frappés (iced Nescafé), *freddo espresso*, *fredd-cino*, and *freddo Mokka.*

Eating

	Price	
IN THE PLAKA **Touristy joints on the main drag and more authentic-feeling places on the quieter hillside above**		
❶ **To Kafeneio**	$$	Tucked in a lane away from the crowds, with a homey setting, affordable prices, friendly service
❷ **Palia Taverna tou Psara** ("The Old Tavern of Psaras")	$$	Pricey dish-'em-up eatery with atmospheric street seating; live folk music in lower building
❸ **Restaurant Hermion**	$$$	Dressy wicker indulgence in a quiet arcade with inviting outdoor seating and an air-conditioned interior
❹ **Sholarhio Ouzeri Kouklis**	$	Serves only fun, inexpensive *mezedes;* free taste of homemade ouzo with this book
ON MNISIKLEOUS **Dreamy stepped lane below the Acropolis, lined with eateries offering live music and rooftop gardens**		
❺ **Xenios Zeus** (ΞΕΝΙΟΣ ΖΕΥΣ)	$$	Proudly set at the top of the steps, with good, traditional Greek food inside or out on a terrace
❻ **Geros Tou Moria Tavern**	$$	Best-regarded Mnisikleous eatery, with a dining hall, intimate terrace, and tables under the grapevines
NEAR MONASTIRAKI SQUARE **"Souvlaki Row," plus a few non-souvlaki places and the Central Market**		
❼ **Thanasis**	$	Famous for its special kebab that combines ground beef and lamb and their secret blend of seasonings
❽ **Savas**	$	Another old favorite souvlaki place, with a similar menu to Thanasis but a little less character
❾ **Bairaktaris**	$	Dominant souvlaki joint on the square itself, but lesser value than Thanasis and Savas

Hours and Days	Address/Phone
Daily 11:00-1:00 in the morning	Epicharmou 1, tel. 210-324-6916
Daily 11:00-24:00, music generally Thu-Sat from 21:00	Eretheos 16, tel. 210-321-8734
Daily 11:30-24.00	Pandrossou 15, tel. 210-324-7148
Daily 11:00-2:00 in the morning	Tripodon 14, tel. 210-324-7605
Daily 10:00-24:00, closed Nov-Feb	Mnisikleous 37, tel. 210-324-9514
Daily 9:00-3:00 in the morning	Mnisikleous 27, tel. 210-322-1753
Daily 10:00-2:00 in the morning	Mitropoleos 69, tel. 210-324-4705
Daily 10:00-3:00 in the morning	Mitropoleos 86, tel. 210-324-5048
Daily 10:00 until late	Monastiraki Square 2, tel. 201-321-3036

	Price		
NEAR MONASTIRAKI SQUARE (continued)			
⓫ **James Joyce Irish Pub**	$$	Woody escape from Greece with Irish-pub ambience and menu, and top Irish beers on tap	
⓬ **Dia Tauta** (a.k.a. Dai Tafta)	$$	Across from the Ancient Agora; try the yummy *bouyiourdi*—veggies baked with feta cheese and chili pepper	
⓭ **Central Market**	$	Great place to assemble a cheap picnic of fruits, veggies, olives, cheeses, nuts, meats, and fish	
⓮ **Soros Grocery Store**	$	Well-stocked enough for a decent picnic	
NEAR SYNTAGMA SQUARE **Urban dining on and near Athens' main square**			
⓯ **O Tzitzikas ki o Mermigkas** ("The Ant and the Cricket")	$$	Updated regional cuisine served at sidewalk tables or indoors in a fun, retro-grocery-store atmosphere	
⓰ **Ariston** (ΑΡΙΣΤΟΝ)	$	Cheapest hot meal in town; Athens' top spot for savory and sweet pastries such as *spanakopita* and *tiropita*	
⓱ **Noodle Bar**	$	A break from Greek fare, with tasty pan-Asian dishes in a small, informal, indoor-outdoor setting	
⓲ **Hotel Grande Bretagne's Roof Garden Restaurant**	$$$	Athens' finest dining experience, on a rooftop garden with spectacular Acropolis/city views; reservations required, dress code	
IN PSYRRI **Thriving nightlife district with eateries concentrated near Iroon and Agii Anargiri squares**			
⓳ **Taverna tou Psyrri**	$$	Old and authentic-feeling, with red-and-white-checkerboard tablecloths, straightforward menu, and good prices	
⓴ **Ivis Cafeneio**	$	Tiny corner ouzo pub run with a passion for tradition; limited Greek-only menu of modern Mediterranean dishes	
㉑ **Pagotomania**	$	Hard to miss—or resist, with a display case bursting with colorful mounds of tasty ice cream	

Hours and Days	Address/Phone
Open daily 10:00 until late	Astingos 12, tel. 210-323-5055
Daily 9:30-1:30 in the morning	Adrianou 37, tel. 210-321-2347
Mon–Sat 7:00–15:00, closed Sun	500 yards north of Monastiraki Square on Athinas street
Daily 8:00-22:00	Mitropoleos 78, tel. 210-322-6677
Mon-Sat 13:00-1:00 in the morning, Sun 13:00-23:00	Mitropoleos 12-14, tel. 210-324-7607
Mon-Sat 7:30-18:00, until 21:00 on Tue-Wed and Fri, closed Sun	Voulis 10, tel. 210-322-7626
Daily 12:00-24:00	Apollonos 1, tel. 210-331-8585
Daily 13:00-1:00 in the morning	North side of Syntagma Square, tel. 210-333-0766
Daily 13:00-24:00	Eshilou 12, tel. 210-321-4923
Daily 13:00-24:00	Corner of Ivis and Navarhou Apostoli just off Ermou, tel. 210-323-2554
Open long hours daily	Corner of Taki and Esopou, tel. 210-323-0001

	Price		
IN THISSIO Hip cafés, cocktail bars, and nightclubs along a strollable pedestrian lane			
㉒ **Filistro** (Φίλιστρο)	$$	On a tranquil stretch of the Apostolou Pavlou promenade; offers one of the best view dining experiences in Athens	
IN MAKRIGIANNI AND KOUKAKI Pair of neighborhoods near the Acropolis Museum, filled with tourist-friendly eateries			
㉓ **Mani Mani**	$$	A nice change of pace, with cuisine from the Mani Peninsula and all-indoor seating (a good bad-weather option)	
㉔ **Strofi Athenian Restaurant**	$$	My favorite for white-tablecloth, elegantly modern, rooftop-Acropolis-view dining; dinner reservations smart	
㉕ **To Kati Allo Restaurant**	$	Quintessential hole-in-the-wall on far side of the Acropolis Museum; blackboard menu lists cheap and tasty options	

Hours and Days	Address/Phone
Tue-Sun 12:00-24:00, July-Aug from 18:00, closed Mon	Apostolou Pavlou 23, tel. 210-342-2897
Tue-Sat 13:00-17:30 & 20:00-24:00, Sun 13:00-17:30, closed Mon	Upstairs at Falirou 10, tel. 210-921-8180
Daily 12:00-24:00	Rovertou Galli 25, tel. 210-921-4130
Open daily	Just off Makrigianni street at Chatzichristou 12, tel. 210-922-3071

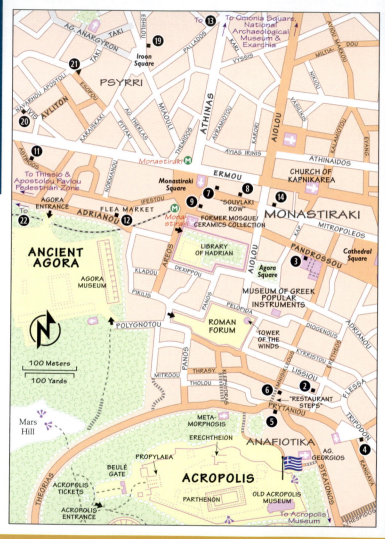

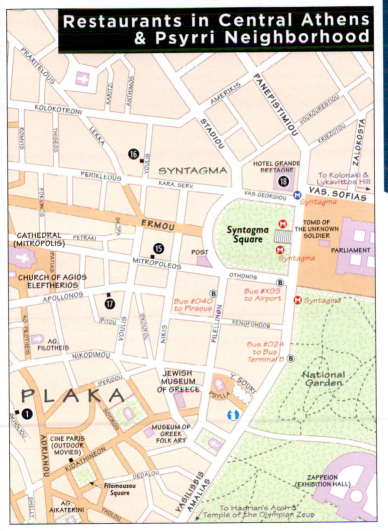

Restaurants in Central Athens & Psyrri Neighborhood

PRAXITELOUS
KOLOKOTRONI
KARTZI
ANTHIMOS
ROMVIS
THISEOS
LEKKA
PERIKLEOUS
FOKINOS
STADIOU
AMERIKIS
PANEPISTIMIOU
VOUKOURESTIOU
KRIEZOTOU
ZALOKOSTA

16

SYNTAGMA

VOULIS

KARA. SERV.

HOTEL GRANDE BRETAGNE

18

VAS.GEORGIOU

To Kolonaki & Lykavittos Hill

VAS. SOFIAS

Ⓜ Syntagma

ERMOU

SKOPA

Syntagma Square

Ⓜ

TOMB OF THE UNKNOWN SOLDIER

Ⓜ Syntagma

PARLIAMENT

CATHEDRAL (MITROPOLIS)

PETRAKI

IPATIAS

15

MITROPOLEOS

POST

OTHONOS

Ⓑ

Bus #X95 to Airport

Ⓜ Syntagma

CHURCH OF AGIOS ELEFTHERIOS

APOLLONOS

17

IPITOU

VOULIS

SKOUFOU

NIKIS

FILELLINON

Bus #040 to Piraeus Ⓑ

XENOFONDOS

AG. FILOTHEIS

AG. FILOTHEIS

NIKODIMOU

Bus #024 to Bus Terminal B Ⓑ

National Garden

IPERIDOU

JEWISH MUSEUM OF GREECE

V. SOUTSOU

P L A K A

SCHOLIOU

1

SOTIROS

MUSEUM OF GREEK FOLK ART

PSYLLA

ℹ

ADRIANOU

CINE PARIS (OUTDOOR MOVIES)

KIDATHINEON

DEDALOU

AG. AIKATERINI

SHELLY

THOLOU

Filomousou Square

VASILISSIS AMALIAS

ZAPPEION (EXHIBITION HALL)

To Hadrian's Arch & Temple of the Olympian Zeus

Eating

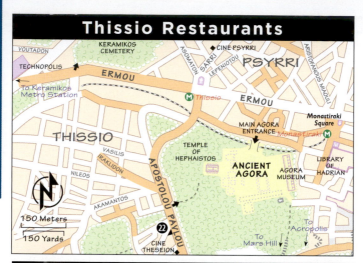

Thissio Restaurants

- VOUTADON
- KERAMIKOS CEMETERY
- CINE PSYRRI
- TECHNOPOLIS
- PSYRRI
- ASOMATON
- SARRI
- LEPENIOTOU
- ARISTOPHANOUS MIAOULI
- ERMOU
- To Keramikos Metro Station
- Thissio
- ERMOU
- Monastiraki Square
- THISSIO
- MAIN AGORA ENTRANCE
- Monastiraki
- VASILIS
- IRAKLIDON
- NILEOS
- TEMPLE OF HEPHAISTOS
- ANCIENT AGORA
- AGORA MUSEUM
- LIBRARY OF HADRIAN
- APOSTOLOU PAVLOU
- AKAMANTOS
- N
- 150 Meters
- 150 Yards
- 22
- CINE THESEION
- To Mars Hill
- To Acropolis

Makrigianni & Koukaki Restaurants

- To Acropolis
- DIONYSIOU AREOPAGITOU
- To Plaka
- N
- 150 Meters
- 150 Yards
- ROVERTOU
- KALLISPERI
- Akropoli
- TZIREON
- MAKRI
- GARIVALDI
- 24
- MAKRIGIANNI
- GALLI
- MITSEON
- ACROPOLIS MUSEUM
- Makrigianni
- FORNOU
- Filopappos Hill
- PROPYLEON
- ERECTHIOU
- RATZIERI
- MISARALIOTOU
- ZITROU
- CHATZICHRISTOU
- STRATEON
- LEMBESI
- PORINOU
- IOSIF TON ROGON
- FILOPAPPOS MONUMENT
- SOFRONISKOU
- PARTHENONOS
- KARATASI
- 25
- LIAKOU
- DRAKOU
- TZAMI
- RENDI
- VEIKOU
- 23
- ANDREA SYNGROU
- PETMEZA
- KORYZI
- VOURVAHI
- THEODOROU
- NEGRI
- MOUSON
- MARKOU BOTSARI
- GONI
- NOTI BOTSARI
- FALIROU
- KALLIRROIS
- TZAMI KARATASI
- KARATZA
- ZAHARITSA
- ANASTASIOU
- ZINNI
- NIKOLAOU DIMITRAKOPOULOU
- ANDROUTSOU
- Syngrou-Fix
- THEOKRITOU
- SISMANI
- IRAKLEOUS
- FILOPAPPOU
- GOUFIE
- VEIKOU
- ODYSSEOS
- FALIROU
- INGLESI
- ALTHOU
- KOUKAKI
- KYNO-SARGOUS

Practicalities

Helpful Websites

Greece's Tourist Information: www.visitgreece.gr

Athens Info: Hellenic Ministry of Culture & Tourism (www.culture .gr); City of Athens Tourism (www.breathtakingathens.com); Matt Barrett's Athens Survival Guide (www.athensguide.com)

Cheap Flights: Olympic (www.olympicairlines.com), Aegean (www .aegeanair.com), or try www.kayak.com

Greek Bus Help (unofficial): http://livingingreece.gr/2008/06/13 /ktel-buses-of-greece

Ferry Schedules for Greek Islands: www.openseas.gr, www.danae .gr/ferries-Greece.asp, www.greekferries.gr

General Travel Tips: www.ricksteves.com (trip planning, packing lists, and more—plus updates for this book)

PLANNING

When to Go

Late spring and fall are pleasant, with comfortable weather, no rain, and lighter crowds (except during holiday weekends). In summer, Athens is packed with tourists, and hotel prices can be high. July and August are the hottest months. Late October through mid-March is colder and can be rainy: During these months, some sights close for lunch and some tourist activities vanish altogether. Off-season hotel rates are soft; look for bargains.

Before You Go

Make sure your passport is up to date (to renew, see www.travel.state .gov). Call your debit- and credit-card companies about your plans (see below). Book hotel rooms in advance, especially for travel during peak season or around any major holidays. Consider buying travel insurance (see www.ricksteves.com/insurance). If traveling beyond Athens, research transit schedules (buses, ferries) and car rentals. If renting a car, you're technically required to have an International Driving Permit (sold at your local AAA office), though I've often rented cars in Greece without one.

MONEY

Greece uses the euro currency: 1 euro (€) = about $1.40. To convert prices in euros to dollars, add about 40 percent: €20 = about $28, €50 = about $70. (Check www.oanda.com for the latest exchange rates.)

Withdraw money from a cash machine using a debit card, just like at home. Visa and MasterCard are commonly used throughout Europe. Before departing, call your bank and credit-card company: Confirm that your card will work overseas, ask about international transaction fees, and alert them that you'll be making withdrawals in Europe.

Be aware that while American credit cards are accepted almost everywhere in Europe, they will not work in some European automated payment machines. Instead, pay with cash, try your PIN code (ask your credit-card company or use a debit card), or find a nearby cashier who should be able to process the transaction.

To keep your valuables safe, wear a money belt. But if you do lose your credit or debit card, report the loss immediately. Call these 24-hour US numbers collect: Visa (410/581-9994), MasterCard (636/722-7111), and American Express (623/492-8427).

ARRIVAL IN ATHENS

Eleftherios Venizelos International Airport

Athens' airport is at Spata, 17 miles east of downtown (tel. 210-353-0000, www.aia.gr). B gates serve European/Schengen countries (no passport control), while A gates cover other destinations, including the US. Both sections feed into a main terminal building (with baggage claim, ATMs, shops, car-rental counters, and info desks).

To get between the airport and downtown Athens, you have several options:

Metro: Line 3/blue zips you downtown (Syntagma or Monastiraki stop) in 45 minutes (2/hour, usually departs at :03 and :33 after the hour, daily 6:00-23:30; €8, ticket good for 1.5 hours on other Athens transit). From the main terminal, use exit #3, cross the street, escalate to the sky-bridge, walk to the station to buy tickets, and follow *Metro* signs to the platforms.

Athens Transit

Metro Line 1
Metro Line 2
Metro Line 3
Bus Line w/#
Rail
Central Athens

Trains to All Over Greece
Kifissia
Irini
Bus Terminal B (Liosion)
Agios Antonios
#024
To Piraeus
#X96
AIRPORT
Aghia Marina
Attiki
Victoria
NATIONAL ARCHAEOLOGICAL MUSEUM
Egaleo
Larissis (Train Stn.)
Bus Terminal A (Kifissou)
Kera-mikos
Omonia
LYKAVITTOS HILL
To Airport
#051
Evangelismos
#X95
#X96
Monastiraki
Thissio
ACROPOLIS
Akropoli
Syntagma
Piraeus
Neo Faliro
#040
Syngrou-Fix
Neos Kosmos
CRUISE PORT
NEA SMYRNI
Saronic Gulf
Agios Dimitrios
Ferries & Hydrofoils to Islands
DCH
Not to Scale

Bus: Express bus #X95 operates 24 hours daily between the airport and Syntagma Square (3-5/hour, 1-1.5 hours depending on traffic, €5, catch it outside exit #5, tel. 185, www.oasa.gr).

Taxi: A taxi stand outside exit #3 offers fixed-price transfers that include all fees (€40 to central Athens).

Bus Stations

Athens' two major bus stations—Kifissou (Terminal A) and Liosion (Terminal B)—are far from downtown and lack convenient Metro connections.

Terminal A, about three miles northwest of the city center, serves buses from the south, including the Peloponnese. To reach central Athens,

Port of Piraeus

Piraeus, six miles southwest of central Athens, is the main port for cruise ships and boats to/from the Greek islands. The easy, cheap way to get between the port and central Athens is by Metro. Line 1/green links Piraeus with the Monastiraki stop in downtown Athens in about 20 minutes (watch for pickpockets on this line, and wear a money belt). Transfer at Omonia for Syntagma, Akropoli, and Syngrou-Fix Metro stops.

A taxi between central Athens and Piraeus costs €10-20 (surcharges apply) and takes 20 minutes to an hour, depending on traffic and start/end points.

Cruise-ship passengers unload at the far-south end of the port. Because the Metro station is a 15-30-minute walk from here, ask at the terminal about public bus #040 or one of the hop-on, hop-off buses that goes to Athens (www.citysightseeing.gr or www.athens-citytour.com).

Practicalities

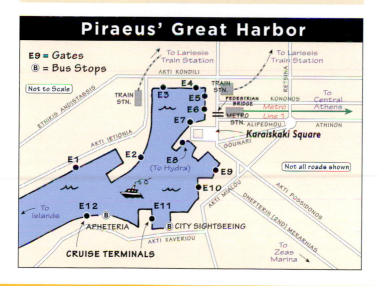

it's easiest to take a taxi (pay no more than €12).

Terminal B, which serves Delphi and other destinations in the north, is about a 15-minute, €8 taxi ride to the Plaka. Bus #024 links Terminal B to Syntagma Square.

Larissis Train Station

Most trains use Larissis Station, just north of downtown (on Metro line 2/red). Eventually, the Acharnes Railway Center (abbreviated SKA), currently under construction 13 miles north of the city center, will become Athens' rail hub.

HELPFUL HINTS

Tourist Information (TI): The Greek National Tourist Organization (EOT), with its main branch near the Acropolis Museum, covers Athens and the rest of the country. Pick up their handy city map, the helpful *Athens City Guide* booklet, and their slick, glossy book on Athens (all free). Although their advice can be hit-or-miss, they do have stacks of informative hand-outs on museums, entertainment options, bus and train connections, and much more (April-Oct Mon-Fri 8:00-20:00, Sat-Sun 10:00-16:00; Nov-March Mon-Fri 9:00-19:00, Sat-Sun 10:00-16:00; on pedestrian street leading to Acropolis Museum at Dionysiou Areopagitou 18-20, Metro line 2/red: Akropoli; tel. 210-331-0392, www.visitgreece.gr, info@gnto.gr).

Hurdling the Language Barrier: Although the Greek alphabet presents challenges to foreign visitors, communication is not hard. Most people in the tourist industry—and virtually all young people—speak English. Many signs and menus use both the Greek and Latin alphabets. For Greek survival phrases, see page 173.

Time Zones: Greece is generally one hour ahead of continental Europe and seven/ten hours ahead of the East/West Coasts of the US.

Watt's Up? Europe's electrical system is 220 volts, instead of North America's 110 volts. Most newer electronics (including hair dryers, lap-tops, and battery chargers) convert automatically, so you won't need a voltage converter—but you will need a special adapter plug with two round prongs, sold inexpensively at US and Canadian travel stores.

Numbers and Stumblers: What Americans call the second floor of a building is the first floor in Europe. Europeans write dates as day/

Tipping

Tipping in Europe isn't as automatic and generous as it is in the US. At Greek restaurants that have waitstaff, service is generally included, although it's common to round up the bill after a good meal (usually 5-10 percent). At hotels, it's polite to give porters a euro for each bag (another reason to pack light). If you like to tip maids, leave a couple of euros in your room at the end of your stay. To tip a taxi driver, add about 5-10 percent.

month/year, so Christmas is 25/12/12. Commas are decimal points and vice versa—a dollar and a half is 1,50, and there are 5.280 feet in a mile.

Greece uses the metric system: A kilogram is 2.2 pounds; a liter is about a quart; and a kilometer is six-tenths of a mile. Temperature is measured in Celsius. 0°C = 32°F. To convert Celsius to Fahrenheit, double the number and add 30.

Holidays: Many sights and banks close down on national holidays. Verify dates through the Greek National Tourist Organization (www.visit greece.gr), or check www.ricksteves.com/festivals.

Pedestrian Safety: Streets that appear to be "traffic-free" often are shared by motorcycles or mopeds. Don't step into any street without looking both ways. Athens' marble-like streets and red pavement tiles can become very slick when it rains. Watch your step.

Internet Access: Bits and Bytes is in the heart of the Plaka (open 24 hours daily, just off Agora Square at Kapnikareas 19, tel. 210-325-3142). **Ivis Travel** is at Syntagma Square (daily 8:00-22:00, upstairs at Mitropoleos 3, tel. 210-324-3365).

Bookshops: Eleftheroudakis (ΕΛΕΥΘΕΡΟΥΔΑΚΗΣ) is Greece's answer to Barnes & Noble, with a great selection of travel guides and maps, along with a lot of English books (Mon-Fri 9:00-21:00, Sat 9:00-18:00, closed Sun, 3 blocks north of Syntagma Square at Panepistimiou/ Eleftheriou Venizelou 15, tel. 210-323-3861 or 210-323-3862, www.books. gr). **Public** at Syntagma Square offers a reasonable variety of English books (tel. 210-324-6210, www.public.gr).

Laundry: A full-service launderette is in the Plaka (closed Sat-Sun, Apollonos 17, tel. 210-323-2226). **Athens Studios,** in the Makriganni neighborhood, operates a self-service launderette (daily, Veikou 3A, tel. 210-922-4044).

GETTING AROUND ATHENS

Because the tourists' core of Athens is so walkable, most travelers don't need the Metro or buses, other than for reaching farther-flung destinations (such as the airport or National Archaeological Museum). For information on all of Athens' public transportation, see www.oasa.gr. Beware of pickpockets.

Buying Tickets

Purchase tickets at machines or from ticket windows. The basic ticket (€1.40) is good for 1.5 hours on all public transit, including the Metro and buses, and covers transfers (excludes trips to the airport). A 24-hour ticket is €4; a one-week ticket costs €14. A one-way bus-only ticket is €1.20 (buy in advance, either from a special ticket kiosk or at a newsstand).

By Metro

The slick Metro is the most straightforward way to get around. Trains run about every five minutes (Sun-Thu 5:00-24:20, Fri-Sat 5:00-2:20 in the morning, www.amel.gr). To avoid a hefty fine, stamp your ticket in a validation machine—usually located near the ticket booth—before you board (24-hour and one-week tickets only need to be stamped the first time).

Athens has three Metro lines. The older and slower **Line 1** (green) stops at Piraeus (boats to the islands), Thissio (good restaurants and nightlife), Monastiraki (city center), Victoria (10-minute walk from National Archaeological Museum), and Irini (Olympic Stadium). Key **Line 2** (red) stops include Larissis (train station), Syntagma (city center), Akropoli (Acropolis and Makrigianni/Koukaki hotel neighborhood), and Syngrou-Fix (Makrigianni/Koukaki hotels). **Line 3** (blue) stops at Keramikos (near Gazi), Monastiraki and Syntagma (city center), Evangelismos (Kolonaki museum neighborhood), and the airport (requires a separate ticket—see page 159).

By Bus

Validate tickets in the orange machines as you board. In general, I'd avoid the slow, crowded buses, with these exceptions: bus #035 (from Athinas street, near Monastiraki, to National Archaeological Museum); bus #224 (from Syntagma Square to National Archaeological Museum); bus #X95 (from airport to Syntagma Square); and bus #X96 (from airport to Piraeus).

By Taxi

Despite the vulgar penchant cabbies here have for ripping off tourists, Athens is a great taxi town. Its yellow taxis are cheap and handy (€3.20 minimum charge covers most short rides in town; after that, it's €0.68/km, plus tolls, fees for bags over 10 kilograms/22 pounds, and surcharges for trips to/from the train and bus stations, airport, and Piraeus). You'll pay double between midnight and 5:00 in the morning (tariff 2) and outside the city limits. Hotels and restaurants can order you a cab for a €2 surcharge (if cabbies try to charge more than €2, hold firm). Note that Athens' cabbies double up, picking up extra passengers headed the same way (though the fare is not shared). Hail any taxi, empty or not.

COMMUNICATING

Telephones

Making Calls: To call Greece from the US or Canada: Dial 011-30 and then the local number (011 is our international access code; 30 is Greece's country code).

To call Greece from a European country: Dial 00-30 followed by the local number (00 is Europe's international access code).

To call within Greece: Just dial the local number (Greece does not use area codes).

To call from Greece to another country: Dial 00, the country code (for example, 1 for the US or Canada), the area code, and number. If you're calling European countries whose phone numbers begin with 0, you'll usually have to omit that 0 when you dial.

Phoning Inexpensively: There are no coin-op phones in Greece— you'll need a prepaid phone card. For local calls from public pay phones, use an insertable *Telekarta* (ΤΗΛΕΚΑΡΤΑ), sold at TIs, tobacco shops, newsstands, post offices, and train stations. To make cheap worldwide calls from your hotel-room phone, get an international phone card; to make

Useful Phone Numbers

Police: tel. 100
Tourist Police: tel. 171 (English-speaking)
Medical or Other Emergency: tel. 112
Ambulance or Fire: tel. 176 or 199
Directory Assistance for Greece: tel. 11880
Directory Assistance for International Calls: tel. 139
US Embassy: tel. 210-720-2414; for after-hours emergency help, tel. 210-729-4444
Canadian Embassy: tel. 210-727-3400; for after-hours emergency help, call Canada collect at tel. 1-613-996-8885

international calls from pay phones, get a Smile+Web card. Purchase international phone cards at newsstands, electronics stores, and long-distance shops.

Mobile Phones: A mobile phone—whether your own from home if it'll work in Greece or a European one you buy upon arrival—is increasingly affordable. You'll find mobile-phone stores selling cheap models with prepaid minutes and SIM cards at the airport and all over Athens. Try the electronics store Germanos (ΓΕΡΜΑΜΟΣ).

Many smartphones work in Europe—but beware of sky-high fees for data downloading (checking email, browsing the Internet, watching videos). Using Wi-Fi is cheaper.

For more on the fast-changing world of telephones, talk to your service provider and see www.ricksteves.com/phoning.

Internet Access

Many hotels offer some form of Internet access—either a computer in the lobby or Wi-Fi (if you bring your own device). Otherwise, your hotelier can point you to the nearest Internet café.

Laptop and smartphone users can make phone calls to other computers and telephones for free or cheaply using applications such as Skype, Google Talk, or FaceTime.

Snail Mail

The most convenient post office is at Syntagma Square (open daily, bottom of the square, at corner with Mitropoleos). Smaller offices (shorter hours, closed Sat-Sun) are in Monastiraki (Mitropoleos 58) and Makrigianni (Dionysiou Areopagitou 7).

SIGHTSEEING TIPS

Information and Hours Alert: Between strikes, budget cuts, and general unpredictability, it's a good idea to confirm hours by calling ahead, asking at the TI, or checking with your hotelier. Ancient sights can abruptly switch between longer "summer" hours and shorter "winter" hours. If you're traveling in the off-season (mid-Sept-late April), visit these sites in the morning, when they're more likely to be open. The Hellenic Ministry of Culture & Tourism's website (www.culture.gr) has information on virtually all the major sights (but be aware that the website might not reflect unexpected changes or closures).

What to Expect: Important sights have metal detectors or conduct bag searches that will slow your entry. Others require you to check (for free) daypacks and coats. To avoid checking a small backpack, carry it under your arm like a purse as you enter. Photos and videos are normally allowed, but flashes or tripods usually are not.

Audioguides are rare in Greece, but at major sights you can usually hire a local guide at a reasonable cost. Prices are negotiable; save money by splitting the fee with other travelers.

Ancient Sights: Archaeological sites are meticulously monitored. Don't cross any barriers or climb on ruins. Posing with ancient statues—or even standing next to them for a photo—is strictly forbidden.

Many major sights have both an archaeological site and a museum. Visiting the museum (artifacts and scale models) helps you imagine the ruins in their heyday; touring the site gives you the lay of the land. I like to see the site first, but crowds and weather can help determine your plan.

Churches: Many churches have divine art and free entry. Churches encourage a modest dress code (no shorts, bare shoulders, or miniskirts), but few enforce it.

Discounts: Many sights offer discounts for seniors, families, and students or teachers with proper identification cards (www.isic.org). Always ask. Children under 18 sometimes get in for free or cheap. Some discounts are only for EU citizens.

Rick Steves' Free Audio Tours: I've produced free, self-guided audio versions of my tours of the Acropolis, Ancient Agora, and National Archaeological Museum, as well as my Athens City Walk (download them via www.ricksteves.com/audioeurope, iTunes, or the Rick Steves Audio Europe free smartphone app).

THEFT AND EMERGENCIES

Theft

While violent crime is rare in the city center, thieves (mainly pickpockets) thrive in crowds, on the main streets through the Plaka (such as Adrianou and Pandrossou), at the Monastiraki flea market, on major public transit routes (such as the Metro between the city and Piraeus), and at the port. Be alert to the possibility of theft, even when you're absorbed in the wonder and newness of Athens. Be on guard when crowds press together, especially at tourist sights; while you're preoccupied at ticket windows; and while boarding and leaving buses and subways. Assume that any beggar or friendly petitioner is really a pickpocket, and any commotion in the crowd is a distraction by a team of thieves. I keep my valuables—passport, credit cards, crucial documents, and large amounts of cash—in a money belt that I tuck under my beltline.

Single male travelers should stay away from bars recommended by strangers encountered on the street. Multilingual con men prowl Syntagma Square and the Plaka looking to coerce their "new friends" into paying for bottles of overpriced champagne.

Emergency Help: If you run into trouble, call the Tourist Police for 24-hour help (tel. 171). They serve as a contact point between tourists and other branches of the police and can also handle disputes with hotels and restaurants (office open 24 hours daily, south of the Acropolis in Koukaki at Veikou 43-45, tel. 210-920-0724).

Lost or Stolen Items: To replace a passport, go to an embassy or consulate (for contact info, see page 166). File a police report without delay; it's required to submit an insurance claim for lost or stolen railpasses or travel gear, and can help with replacing your passport or credit and debit cards. For more information, see www.ricksteves.com/help.

Medical Help

Dial 112 for a medical emergency. If you get sick, do as the Greeks do and go to a pharmacy, where qualified technicians routinely diagnose and prescribe medication and treatments. Or ask at your hotel for help—they'll know the nearest medical and emergency services should you need to see a doctor.

ACTIVITIES

Shopping

Most shops catering to tourists are open long hours daily. Those serving locals generally open Monday-Saturday at 8:30 or 9:00 (closed on Sunday); they close in the early afternoon on Monday, Wednesday, and Saturday (between 14:30 and 16:00), but tend to stay open late on Tuesday, Thursday, and Friday (until 20:00 or 21:00), often with an afternoon break (around 14:00-17:00 or 18:00).

Shopping Neighborhoods: The main streets of the Plaka—especially Adrianou and Pandrossou—are crammed with crass tourist-trap shops (with room to bargain, especially if buying several items).

The famous Monastiraki flea market—selling fake designer clothes, antiques, dusty books, and other junk—stretches west of Monastiraki Square, along Ifestou street and its side streets (daily, best on Sun 8:00-15:00).

For upscale shopping at mostly international chain stores, stroll the pedestrianized Ermou street between Syntagma Square and Monastiraki. Even fancier boutiques are in the swanky Kolonaki area.

To shop like an Athenian, check out the streets just to the north of Ermou street—including Perikleous, Lekka, and Kolokotroni. ZOYΛOBITS (Zoulovits) is the Greek answer to Tiffany's (at Perikleous 10); for cheaper alternatives, visit the silver-and-jewelry gift shops on Lekka street.

What and Where to Buy: Serious buyers tell me that Athens is the best place in Greece to purchase fine jewelry, particularly at the shops along Adrianou (haggling OK). Melissinos Art, the famous "poet sandal-maker" of Athens, sells leather sandals (just off Monastiraki Square at the edge of Psyrri, Ag. Theklas 2). The Institute of Social Protection and Solidarity Arts & Crafts Shop has a good selection of Greek carpets made by rural women; profits help preserve traditional handicrafts (a block from the TI near Syntagma Square at Filellinon 14). Loosely based on prayer beads, worry beads make for a fun Greek souvenir and are sold all over central Athens.

Sizes: European clothing sizes are different from those in the US. For example, a woman's size 10 dress (US) is a European size 40, and a size 8 shoe (US) is a European size 38-39.

Getting a VAT Refund: If you spend more than €120 on goods at a single store, you may be eligible to get a refund of the 23 percent Value-Added Tax (VAT). You'll need to ask the merchant to fill out the necessary refund document, then process your refund through a service such as Global Blue or Premier Tax Free, with offices at major airports. For more details, see www.ricksteves.com/vat.

Customs for American Shoppers: You are allowed to take home $800 worth of items per person duty-free, once every 30 days. You can also bring in a liter of alcohol duty-free. As for food, you can take home many processed and packaged foods (e.g. vacuum-packed cheeses, chocolate, mustard) but no fresh produce or meats. Any liquid-containing foods must be packed (carefully) in checked luggage. To check customs rules and duty rates, visit www.cbp.gov.

Nightlife

Athens is a thriving, vibrant city...and Athenians know how to have a good time after hours. For events, look for *Life in Capital A* and *Athens Today* (both free from the TI), the weekly English-language *Athens News,* the *Athens Plus* newspaper, and the Greek lifestyle magazine *Odyssey.*

Nightlife Neighborhoods: Your best bet is to get out of the touristy Plaka/Monastiraki rut. In Thissio, just beyond the Agora, the tables and couches of trendy clubs and cocktail bars clog pedestrian lanes under a gleaming Acropolis. In seedy-chic Psyrri (immediately north of Thissio), crumbling, graffiti-slathered buildings coexist with hip nightclubs, touristy tavernas with live traditional music, and highly conceptual café/bars. Gazi—the center of Athens' gay community—has a special flamboyance and style.

Strolling: *The* place for an evening stroll is the pedestrian boulevard arcing around the base of the Acropolis—what I call the "Acropolis Loop" (see page 122).

Outdoor Cinema: Screenings, which take place most nights in summer, come with folding chairs and small tables for your drinks (roughly

June-Sept, sometimes in May and Oct). Try one of these venues: Aigli Village Cinema (at the Zappeion in the National Garden, tel. 210-336-9369), Cine Paris (in the Plaka, overlooking Filomousou Square on the roof of Kidathineon 22, tel. 210-324-8057, www.cineparis.gr), Cine Psyrri (Sarri 44, near intersection with Ogigou, tel. 210-324-7234), and Cine Theseion (in Thissio at Apostolou Pavlou 7, tel. 210-347-0980, www.cine-thisio.gr).

Folk Dancing: The Dora Stratou Theater hosts Greece's best folk-dance company (late May-late Sept, daily except Mon, on southern side of Filopappos Hill, tel. 210-324-4395, after 19:30 call 210-921-4650, www.grdance.org).

Festivals: Athens' biggest party is the Athens & Epidavros Festival, highlighted by performances at the Odeon of Herodes Atticus. Tickets for the June-July festival generally go on sale three weeks in advance; same-day tickets are also sold at the theater box office (Mon-Fri 8:30-16:00, Sat 9:00-14:30, closed Sun, in the arcade at Panepistimiou 39, opposite the National Library, tel. 210-327-2000).

Tours

Bus Tours: The well-regarded Hop In (tel. 210-428-5500, www.hopin.com), CHAT Tours (tel. 210-323-0827, www.chatours.gr), Key Tours (tel. 210-923-3166, www.keytours.gr), and GO Tours (tel. 210-921-9555, www.gotours.com.gr) offer tours within and outside of Athens. Various options are a bus-plus-walking tour of Athens (with guided Acropolis visit); a night city tour that finishes with dinner and folk dancing at a taverna; and day-long tours to Delphi and to Mycenae, Nafplio, and Epidavros.

Hop-on, Hop-off Bus Tours: For a city overview and an easy way to reach outlying sights, consider hop-on, hop-off buses from City Sightseeing Athens (€18, tel. 210-922-0604, www.citysightseeing.gr) or Athens City Tour (€15, tel. 210-881-5207, www.athensopenbus.com). The main stop for both is on Syntagma Square, or look for signs around town.

Tourist Trains: Two trains do a sightseeing circuit through Athens' tourist zone. Catch the Sunshine Express on Aiolou street along the Hadrian's Library fence at Agora Square (€5, 40-minute loop, departs hourly May-Sept daily, Oct-April Sat-Sun only, www.sunshine-express.gr). The Athens Happy Train stops at the bottom of Syntagma Square, at Monastiraki Square, and just below the Acropolis (€6, 1-hour loop, 2/hour daily, hop-on, hop-off privileges at strategic stops, www.athenshappytrain.com).

Walking Tours: Athens Walking Tours offers an Acropolis and City Tour (€36 plus entry fees, daily at 9:30, 3 hours, departs from Syntagma Metro station, under hanging clock one level down) and an Acropolis Museum Tour (€29 plus entry fee, Tue-Sun at 13:45, 1.5 hours, meet at museum's cash desk, tel. 210-884-7269, mobile 694-585-9662, www.athenswalkingtours.gr, Despina).

Local Guide: Effie Perperi is a fine private guide (€50/hour, tel. 210-951-2566, mobile 697-739-6659, effieperperi@gmail.com).

RESOURCES FROM RICK STEVES

This Pocket guide is one of more than 30 titles in my series of guide-books on European travel, including *Rick Steves' Greece: Athens & the Peloponnese.* I also produce a public television series, *Rick Steves' Europe,* and a public radio show, *Travel with Rick Steves.*

My website, www.ricksteves.com, offers free travel information, free vodcasts and podcasts of my shows, free audio tours of Europe's great sights, a Graffiti Wall for travelers' comments, guidebook updates, my travel blog, an online travel store, and information on European railpasses and our tours of Europe.

How was your trip? If you'd like to share your tips, concerns, and discoveries after using this book, please fill out the survey at www.ricksteves.com/feedback. It helps us and fellow travelers.

Greek Survival Phrases

Knowing a few phrases of Greek can help if you're traveling off the beaten path. Just learning the pleasantries (such as please and thank you) will improve your connections with locals, even in the bigger cities.

Because Greek words can be transliterated differently in English, I've also included the Greek spellings. Note that in Greek, a semicolon is used the same way we use a question mark.

Hello. (formal)	**Gia sas.**	Γειά σας.	yah sahs
Hi. / Bye. (informal)	**Gia.**	Γειά.	yah
Good morning.	**Kali mera.**	Καλή μέρα.	kah-**lee** meh-rah
Good afternoon.	**Kali spera.**	Καλή σπέρα.	kah-**lee** speh-rah
Do you speak English?	**Milate anglika?**	Μιλάτε αγγλικά;	mee-**lah**-teh ahn-glee-**kah**
Yes. / No.	**Ne. / Ohi.**	Ναι. / Όχι.	neh / **oh**-hee
I understand.	**Katalaveno.**	Καταλαβαίνω.	kah-tah-lah-**veh**-noh
I don't understand.	**Den katalaveno.**	Δεν καταλαβαίνω.	dehn kah-tah-lah-**veh**-noh
Please. (Also: You're welcome.)	**Parakalo.**	Παρακαλώ.	pah-rah-kah-**loh**
Thank you (very much).	**Efharisto (poli).**	Ευχαριστώ (πολύ).	ehf-hah-ree-**stoh** (poh-**lee**)
Excuse me. (Also: I'm sorry.)	**Sygnomi.**	Συγνώμη.	seeg-**noh**-mee
(No) problem.	**(Kanena) problima.**	(Κανένα) πρόβλημα	(kah-**neh**-nah) **prohv**-lee-mah
Good.	**Orea.**	Ωραία.	oh-**reh**-ah
Goodbye.	**Antio.**	Αντίο.	ahd-**yoh** (think "adieu")
Good night.	**Kali nikta.**	Καλή νύχτα.	kah-**lee** neek-**tah**
one / two	**ena / dio**	ένα / δύο	**eh**-nah / **dee**-oh
three / four	**tria / tessera**	τρία / τέσσερα	**tree**-ah / **teh**-seh-rah
five / six	**pente / exi**	πέντε / έξι	**peh**-deh / **ehk**-se
seven / eight	**efta / ohto**	εφτά / οχτώ	ehf-**tah** / oh-**toh**
nine / ten	**ennia / deka**	εννιά / δέκα	ehn-**yah** / **deh**-kah
hundred / thousand	**ekato / hilia**	εκατό / χίλια	eh-kah-**toh** / **heel**-yah
How much?	**Poso kani?**	Πόσο κάνει;	**poh**-soh kah-**nee**
euro	**evro**	ευρώ	ev-**roh**
Write it?	**Grapsete to?**	Γράπσετε το;	**grahp**-seh-teh toh
Is it free?	**Ine dorean?**	Είναι δωρεάν;	**ee**-neh doh-ree-**ahn**
Is it included?	**Perilamvanete?**	Περιλαμβάνεται;	peh-ree-lahm-**vah**-neh-teh
Where can I find / buy...?	**Pou boro na vro / agoraso...?**	Που μπορώ να βρω / αγοράσω...;	poo boh-**roh** nah vroh / ah-goh-**rah**-soh
I'd like / We'd like...	**Tha ithela / Tha thelame...**	Θα ήθελα / Θα θέλαμε...	thah **ee**-theh-lah / thah **theh**-lah-meh
...a room.	**...ena dhomatio.**	...ένα δωμάτιο.	**eh**-nah doh-**mah**-tee-oh

...a ticket to ___.	...ena isitirio gia ___.	...ένα εισιτήριο για ___.	eh-nah ee-see-**tee**-ree-oh yah ___
Is it possible?	Ginete?	Γίνεται;	**yee**-neh-teh
Where is...?	Pou ine...?	Που είναι...;	poo **ee**-neh
...the bus station	...o stathmos ton leoforion	...ο σταθμός των λεωφορίων	oh **stahth**-mohs tohn leh-oh-foh-**ree**-ohn
...the train station	...o stathmos tou trenou	...ο σταθμός του τρένου	oh **stahth**-mohs too **treh**-noo
...the tourist information office	...to grafeio enimerosis touriston	...το γραφείο ενημέρωσης τουριστών	too grah-**fee**-oh eh-nee-**meh**-roh-sis too-ree-**stohn**
...the toilet	...toualeta	...τουαλέτα	twah-**leh**-tah
men	andres	άντρες	**ahn**-drehs
women	gynekes	γυναίκες	yee-**neh**-kehs
left / right	dexia / aristera	δεξιά / αριστερά	dehk-see-**ah** / ah-ree-steh-**rah**
straight	efthia	ευθεία	ehf-**thee**-ah
At what time...	Ti ora...	Τι ώρα...	tee **oh**-rah
...does this open / close?	...anigete / klinete?	...ανοίγετε / κλείνετε;	ah-**nee**-yeh-teh / **klee**-neh-teh
Just a moment.	Ena lepto.	Ένα λεπτό.	**eh**-nah lep-**toh**
now / soon / later	tora / se ligo / argotera	τώρα / σε λίγο / αργότερα	**toh**-rah / seh **lee**-goh / ar-**goh**-teh-rah
today / tomorrow	simera / avrio	σήμερα / αύριο	**see**-meh-rah / **ahv**-ree-oh

In the Restaurant

I'd like to reserve...	Tha ithela na kliso...	Θα ήθελα να κλείσω...	thah **ee**-theh-lah nah **klee**-soh
We'd like to reserve...	Tha thelame na klisoume...	Θα θέλαμε να κλείσουμε...	thah **theh**-lah-meh nah **klee**-soo-meh
...a table for one / two.	...ena trapezi gia enan / dio.	...ένα τραπέζι για έναν / δύο.	eh-nah trah-**peh**-zee yah **eh**-nahn / **dee**-oh
non-smoking	mi kapnizon	μη καπνίζων	mee kahp-**nee**-zohn
Is this table free?	Ine eleftero afto to trapezi?	Είναι ελεύθερο αυτό το τραπέζι;	**ee**-neh eh-**lef**-teh-roh ahf-**toh** toh trah-**peh**-zee
The menu (in English), please.	Ton katalogo (sta anglika) parakalo.	Τον κατάλογο (στα αγγλικά) παρακαλώ.	tohn kah-**tah**-loh-goh (stah ahn-glee-**kah**) pah-rah-kah-**loh**
service (not) included	to servis (den) perilamvanete	το σέρβις (δεν) περιλαμβάνεται	toh **sehr**-vees (dehn) peh-ree-lahm-**vah**-neh-teh
cover charge	kouver	κουβέρ	koo-**vehr**
"to go"	gia exo	για έξω	yah **ehk**-soh
with / without	me / horis	με / χωρίς	meh / hoh-**rees**
and / or	ke / i	και / ή	keh / ee
fixed-price meal	menu	μενού	meh-**noo**

specialty of the house	i specialite tou magaziou	η σπεσιαλιτέ του μαγαζιού	ee speh-see-ah-lee-teh too mah-gah-zee-oo
half-portion	misi merida	μισή μερίδα	mee-see meh-ree-dah
daily special	to piato tis meras	το πιάτο της μέρας	toh pee-ah-toh tees meh-rahs
appetizers	proto piato	πρώτο πιάτο	proh-toh pee-ah-toh
bread	psomi	ψωμί	psoh-mee
cheese	tiri	τυρί	tee-ree
sandwich	sandwich or toast	σάντουιτς, τόστ	"sandwich," "toast"
soup	soupa	σούπα	soo-pah
salad	salata	σαλάτα	sah-lah-tah
meat	kreas	κρέας	kray-ahs
poultry / chicken	poulerika / kotopoulo	πουλερικά / κοτόπουλο	poo-leh-ree-kah / koh-toh-poo-loh
fish / seafood	psari / psarika	ψάρι / ψαρικά	psah-ree / psah-ree-kah
shellfish	thalassina	θαλασσινά	thah-lah-see-nah
fruit	frouta	φρούτα	froo-tah
vegetables	lahanika	λαχανικά	lah-hah-nee-kah
dessert	gliko	γλυκό	lee-koh
(tap) water	nero (tis vrisis)	νερό (της βρύσης)	neh-roh (tees vree-sees)
mineral water	metalliko nero	μεταλλικό νερό	meh-tah-lee-koh neh-roh
milk	gala	γάλα	gah-lah
(orange) juice	himos (portokali)	χυμός (πορτοκάλι)	hee-mohs (por-toh-kah-lee)
coffee	kafes	καφές	kah-fehs
tea	tsai	τσάι	chah-ee
wine (spoken)	krasi	κρασί	krah-see
wine (printed on label)	inos	οίνος	ee-nohs
red / white	kokkino / aspro	κόκκινο / άσπρο	koh-kee-noh / ah-sproh
sweet / dry / semi-dry	gliko / ksiro / imixiro	γλυκό / ξηρό / ημίξηρο	lee-koh / ksee-roh / ee-meek-see-roh
glass / bottle	potiri / boukali	ποτήρι /μπουκάλι	poh-tee-ree / boo-kah-lee
beer	bira	μπύρα	bee-rah
Here you are. (when given food)	Oriste.	Ορίστε.	oh-ree-steh
Enjoy your meal!	Kali orexi!	Καλή όρεξη!	kah-lee oh-rehk-see
(To your) health! (like "Cheers!")	(Stin i) gia mas!	(Στην υ) γειά μας!	(stee nee) yah mahs
Another.	Allo ena.	Άλλο ένα.	ah-loh eh-nah
Bill, please.	Ton logariasmo parakalo.	Τον λογαριασμό παρακαλώ.	tohn loh-gah-ree-ahs-moh pah-rah-kah-loh
tip	bourbouar	μπουρμπουάρ	boor-boo-ar
Very good!	Poli oreo!	Πολύ ωραίο!	poh-lee oh-ray-oh
Delicious!	Poli nostimo!	Πολύ νόστιμο!	poh-lee nohs-tee-moh

INDEX

Start your trip at

Our website enhances this book and turns

Explore Europe

At ricksteves.com you can browse through thousands of articles, videos, photos and radio interviews, plus find a wealth of money-saving travel tips for planning your dream trip. And with our mobile-friendly website, you can easily access all this great travel information anywhere you go.

TV Shows

Preview the places you'll visit by watching entire half-hour episodes of Rick Steves' Europe (choose from all 100 shows) on-demand, for free.

ricksteves.com

your travel dreams into affordable reality

Radio Interviews

Enjoy ready access to Rick's vast library of radio interviews covering  travel tips and cultural insights that relate specifically to your Europe travel plans.

Travel Forums

Learn, ask, share! Our online community of savvy travelers is a great resource for first-time travelers to Europe, as well as seasoned pros. You'll find forums on each country, plus travel tips and restaurant/hotel reviews. You can even ask one of our well-traveled staff to chime in with an opinion.

Travel News

Subscribe to our free Travel News e-newsletter, and get monthly updates from Rick on what's happening in Europe.

Audio Europe™

Rick's Free Travel App

Get your FREE Rick Steves Audio Europe™ app to enjoy…

- Dozens of self-guided tours of Europe's top museums, sights and historic walks
- Hundreds of tracks filled with cultural insights and sightseeing tips from Rick's radio interviews
- All organized into handy geographic playlists
- For Apple and Android

With Rick whispering in your ear, Europe gets even better.

Find out more at ricksteves.com

Pack Light and Right

Gear up for your next adventure at ricksteves.com

Light Luggage

Pack light and right with Rick Steves' affordable, custom-designed rolling carry-on bags, backpacks, day packs and shoulder bags.

Accessories

From packing cubes to moneybelts and beyond, Rick has personally selected the travel goodies that will help your trip go smoother.

Shop at ricksteves.com

Rick Steves has

Experience maximum Europe

Save time and energy

This guidebook is your independent-travel toolkit. But for all it delivers, it's still up to you to devote the time and energy it takes to manage the preparation and logistics that are essential for a happy trip. If that's a hassle, there's a solution.

Rick Steves Tours

A Rick Steves tour takes you to Europe's most interesting places with great guides and small groups

great tours, too!

with minimum stress

of 28 or less. We follow Rick's favorite itineraries, ride in comfy buses, stay in family-run hotels, and bring you intimately close to the Europe you've traveled so far to see. Most importantly, we take away the logistical headaches so you can focus on the fun.

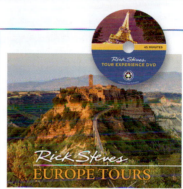

Join the fun

This year we'll take thousands of free-spirited travelers—nearly half of them repeat customers—along with us on 40 different itineraries, from Ireland to Italy to Istanbul. Is a Rick Steves tour the right fit for your travel dreams? Find out at ricksteves.com, where you can also get Rick's latest tour catalog and free Tour Experience DVD.

Europe is best experienced with happy travel partners. We hope you can join us.

See our itineraries at ricksteves.com

Rick Steves

Rick Steves guidebooks are published by Avalon Travel, a member of the Perseus Books Group.

Maximize your travel skills
with a good guidebook.

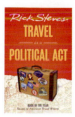

POCKET GUIDES
Amsterdam
Athens
Barcelona
Florence
London
Munich & Salzburg
Paris
Rome
Venice
Vienna

TRAVEL CULTURE
Europe 101
European Christmas
Postcards from Europe
Travel as a Political Act

eBOOKS
Nearly all Rick Steves guides are available as ebooks. Check with your favorite bookseller.

RICK STEVES' EUROPE DVDs
12 New Shows 2015–2016
Austria & the Alps
The Complete Collection 2000–2016
Eastern Europe
England & Wales
European Christmas

European Travel Skills & Specials
France
Germany, BeNeLux & More
Greece, Turkey & Portugal
The Holy Land: Israelis & Palestinians Today
Iran
Ireland & Scotland
Italy's Cities
Italy's Countryside
Scandinavia
Spain
Travel Extras

PHRASE BOOKS & DICTIONARIES
French
French, Italian & German
German
Italian
Portuguese
Spanish

PLANNING MAPS
Britain, Ireland & London
Europe
France & Paris
Germany, Austria & Switzerland
Ireland
Italy
Spain & Portugal

RickSteves.com 🇫 🇹 **@RickSteves**

Rick Steves books are available at bookstores
and through online booksellers.

Photo © Patricia Feaster

PHOTO CREDITS

ABOUT THE AUTHORS

Rick Steves

Rick produces a public television series *(Rick Steves' Europe)* and a public radio show *(Travel with Rick Steves);* writes a bestselling guidebook series and organizes guided tours that take thousands of travelers to Europe annually. Rick's mission is to make European travel fun, affordable, and culturally enlightening for Americans.

Gene Openshaw

Gene is a writer, composer, tour guide, and lecturer on art and history. Specializing in writing walking tours of Europe's cultural sights, Gene is the co-author of 10 Rick Steves' books and contributes to Rick's public television series. He lives near Seattle with his daughter and roots for the Mariners in good times and bad.

Cameron Hewitt

Cameron writes and edits guidebooks for Rick Steves. For this book, he explored Athens' evocative ancient sites and rollicking tavernas—along the way discovering a new favorite dessert *(kataifi).* Cameron lives in Seattle with his wife Shawna.

FOLDOUT COLOR MAP ▶

The foldout map on the opposite page includes:
- Maps of Athens on one side
- Maps of Greece, Athens transit, and the port of Piraeus on the other side

Avalon Travel
a member of the Perseus Books Group
1700 Fourth Street
Berkeley, CA 94710, USA

Printed in China by RR Donnelley
Third printing July 2015
Portions of this book were originally published in *Rick Steves' Best of Europe* © 2006 by Rick Steves and *Rick Steves' Europe Through the Back Door* © 2002, 2003, 2004, 2005, 2006, 2007, 2008 by Rick Steves.

ISBN 978-1-61238-131-2
ISSN 2165-0802

For the latest on Rick's lectures, books, tours, public-radio show, and public-television series, contact Rick Steves' Europe, 130 Fourth Avenue North, Edmonds, WA 98020, tel. 425/771-8303, fax 425/771-0833, www.ricksteves.com, rick@ricksteves.com.

Rick Steves' Europe Head Editor: Cathy Lu
RSE Reviewing Editor: Jennifer Madison Davis
RSE Editors: Gretchen Strauch, Tom Griffin, Cathy McDonald, Suzanne Kotz, Samantha Oberholzer
RSE Managing Editor: Risa Laib
Additional Writing: Gene Openshaw, Cameron Hewitt, David Willett
Research Assistance: Tom Griffin
Avalon Travel Senior Editor & Series Manager: Madhu Prasher
Avalon Travel Project Editor: Kelly Lydick
Copy Editor: Denise Silva
Proofreader: Becca Freed
Indexer: Stephen Callahan
Production & Typesetting: McGuire Barber Design
Cover Design: Kimberly Glyder Design
Graphic Content Director: Laura VanDeventer
Maps and Graphics: David C. Hoerlein, Laura VanDeventer, Lauren Mills, Twozdai Hulse, Kat Bennett, Brice Ticen, Mike Morgenfeld
Front Cover Image: right, Caryatids Portico, figures of the Six Maidens, Erechtheion, Athens, Greece © Guy Thouvenin/Getty Images; left, Ionic Capital © Massimo Pizzotti/Getty Images